Chow! Venice

Savoring the Food and Wine of La Serenissima

A guide to restaurants and bars in Venice

WAG

Shannon Essa and Ruth Edenbaum
Designed by: Paul Zografakis

Published by:

The Wine Appreciation Guild and Chow Bella Books
360 Swift Avenue Suite 34
S. San Francisco, CA 94080
(800) 231-9463
www.wineappreciation.com

Library of Congress Control Number: 2006934677
ISBN: 1-934259-00-4
ISBN: 978-1-934259-00-9
Printed in the United States of America
Layout, Map and Cover Design: Paul Zografakis
Cover Photos: Ruth Edenbaum
Contributing Editor: Nan McElroy

Table OF Contents

Introduction:

Dear Reader,

With this new edition of Chow! Venice, you will see many changes.
Venice has changed, and both of us have experienced firsthand the
culinary renaissance that is going on there. Five years ago, those who
said, "you cannot eat well in Venice" were wrong; now they are REALLY
wrong. New establishments serving classic Venetian cuisine are popping
up all over the place, and there are new wine bars everywhere. Even the
older bars are serving better wine by the glass than they once did, and
Venice, which used to seem like a ghost town after 10:00 p.m., now has
an energetic nighttime scene. It's pretty thrilling for us to see the culinary
scene in Venice grow and thrive.

We would like to touch on a few things before we "get to the Chow."
This book is an intensely personal guide. It is not meant to be the be-all
end-all book, nor the Bible of eating in Venice. We simply wish to point
out to our readers the places that we have enjoyed and continue to enjoy.
As always we appreciate reader comments on our website and by email,
so please do write to us with comments or suggestions. As a buyer of our
book, you can also write to us before your trip with any additional que-
ries. We are always happy to help.

In 2005, within days of each other, Ruth and Martin welcomed grandson
David into this world, and Shannon was blessed with her first nephew,
Ryan. This edition is dedicated to them both, and we can't wait to take
them to Venice and feed them their first tastes of real Italian food in the
city that we all love.

Now, on to the Chow!

Shannon Essa & Ruth Edenbaum

Ruth would like to thank:

Martin for everything especially eating wonderful meals with me, and for his eagle eyed proofreading.

Sarah and *Brian* for also sharing so many meals including one of the worst ever - and extra thanks to Brian for allowing us to benefit from his sommelier's knowledge and palate.

Tom for legal advice, and *Tom* and *Lorena* for giving me a reason - *David* - to come home from Venice.

Gerarda for coming to Venice to be another food taster for Chow! Venice.

All of the above plus *James* and *Dan* for their love and support in regard to the book in particular and life in general.

Shannon would like to thank:

Connie Medhara, Doris Hanson, Tom Essa, Jay Essa, Carrie Macker, Donna Bottrell, and *Elliott Mackey* for their help, love, and support. Not only for this book, but also for helping me be the person I am with the life I live.

We would both like to thank:

Pauline Kenny, Colleen Alley, Leslie Dixon, Nan McElroy, Lucia Vianello, Giovanni Bottaro, Silvia Costa, and the community at Slowtalk.com for a great many suggestions, constant cheerleading, and help with the finished product.

Jason Rosenstock, our webpage designer.

Paul Zografakis, our book designer, who clearly did not know what he was getting into when he took on this project, yet created something beautiful again!

Some Notes about the Book

There are two main sections in this book: the restaurant guide, and the bar guide. Included in the bar guide are several places that could be in either category, but we use them more as bars than as restaurants. If you want to sit down and eat a full meal at one of these establishments, you won't go wrong unless we specifically recommend it as a bar only.

How we chose what we chose: Both of us have spent a lot of time in Venice, and if one of your favorite restaurants has been omitted, it is because we have either not eaten there, or because we have and found it lacking. There are restaurants with rave reviews in some of our favorite guidebooks that left us wondering "huh?" Our picks are places that we go back to again and again, that are consistently good and that treat tourists well.

In this edition there have been some deletions and some additions. In some cases the deleted restaurants have changed hands and changed direction, in others, they have simply failed to adhere to former high standards, and in still others we have found restaurants that we feel offer even better food and/or better value.

Hours of operation and vacation closures: Though we have supplied the days of operation here, trying to keep up on vacation closures is a next to impossible task, as they are constantly changing. In fact, the hours Venetians work vs. what is posted is a complete conundrum to us. Many places are closed for all or parts of January, February and August, so if you are visiting during these months it is always good to call ahead. As for closing times, even if we say a bar is open till 1:00 a.m., it is not unheard of to get there and find it closed up tight. Restaurant hours are generally posted pretty accurately. Most restaurants are open from 12:00 p.m. until 2:30 or 3:00 p.m. for lunch and 7:30 p.m. until 10:30 p.m. for dinner. We have made special notes on places open later.

Credit cards: We have answered this question with a simple yes or no. Mastercard and Visa are taken if we say "yes." Amex is usually accepted, Discover never. Cold, hard cash is the preferred form of payment anywhere in Italy.

Coperto, Tipping and Service: In almost every Italian restaurant you will be charged a small fee *(coperto)* just to sit down, ranging from as little as 1 Euro on up to 4 or 5 Euro in fancier places. A charge for service *(servizio)* is often added to the bill, usually 12%. If the *servizio* is added to your bill, feel free to add a few extra coins if the service was exceptional. If the *servizio* is not added, leave 10-15%. In bars, you can leave small change on the counter as a tip, but you won't be kicked out of Venice if you don't.

Children: Italians love kids, and we have seen children in every sort of place, from bars to pizzerias to fine restaurants. That said, the children in Italy are exceptionally well behaved, but they are used to later eating hours and long waits. It is fine to bring your children to any listing in this book, but if you are going to an expensive restaurant like Da Fiore, it would help if they are used to this kind of upscale, fine dining experience. Be forewarned though, after your kids have tasted pasta in Italy, they aren't going to want the stuff served at Italian "restaurants" near the mall at home.

Maps and directions: We have included walking directions to all the restaurants and bars listed, and there are maps with all listings as well. Usually we start the walking directions from a landmark or vaporetto stop, so look for that location on your map first.

Smoking: There is a new Italian law that bans smoking in public places. Smoking is no longer allowed inside bars and restaurants, but it is allowed at outdoor tables. Some places have zip-up plastic tents to use on rainy days or mild days in the cooler season. Some restaurants consider these "inside" and others "outside" so smoking may or may not be permitted in these. Smokers now smoke in the calli outside many establishments, creating the illusion that the establishment is much more crowded than it actually is.

Paying the bill: When you are ready for your check, ask for *"il conto, per favore."* Sometimes it seems to take forever for it to come, so be prepared to wait. You should always get an itemized bill and check it carefully for mistakes. Italian law requires you, the customer, to have a receipt when you leave any place of business in Italy – if you don't have one, you could be fined. Simply ask for *"la ricevuta, per favore."*

Prices: In each listing there is a price range, but a meal can go from inexpensive to moderate or moderate to expensive very quickly if you order several courses. We hope that the listings themselves will also give you an idea of what to expect when the bill comes. These prices are per person and generally include two courses, water and house wine. Split dishes or order one dish rather than two to knock your meal into the lesser category.

Inexpensive – less than 20 Euro per person
Moderate – 20 - 40 Euro per person
Expensive – 40 - 60 Euro per person
Very expensive – over 60 Euro per person

Other tips: Don't ask for a "doggie bag." It is just not done in Italy. In a pizzeria that offers take-out it is fine to ask for a take-away box. Do not order drinks at a bar and then sit down at a table when there is table service. Never sit down at a café table with your cone of gelato, even if you bought the gelato from what looks to be part of the café.

Italian food terms: There is a glossary at the end of this book.

Updates: Everything changes, so please check our website (*www.chowbellabooks.com*) for up-to-the-minute information on management changes, closures, and comments from our readers that might affect the outcome of a restaurant visit. If you don't have the internet, send us a note and we will mail you an update.

The address is: *Shannon Essa*
c/o W.A.G.
360 Swift Ave. Ste 34,
S. San Francisco, CA 94080

How, When & What
TO Eat IN Venice.

Mornings

Venetians generally eat *prima colazione* (breakfast) like most Italians –
a quick espresso or cappuccino taken with a brioche or pastry, often
consumed standing up at a bar. Italians drink espresso at all times of
the day and night; in fact, the response to a request for *un caffè* is an
espresso. Cappuccino is only ordered by Venetians before 10:30 a.m.
but it is fine (though tourist-like) to do so after this time. It is considered
uncouth to have milk in your coffee in the evening. If you order a *latte*,
be prepared for a glass of steamed milk; order a *caffè latte* if you want
coffee mixed with steamed milk. You will often see a Venetian start the
day with a *caffè corretto* (espresso with a small shot of grappa or other
liquor), or a tumbler of *amaro* (a bitter, herbal digestive). It is not
uncommon to see the first *ombra* (small glass of wine) tossed back as
early as 8:00 a.m., especially in the Rialto market where some of the
vendors have been awake for hours, making 8:00 a.m. considerably
later in their day than it may be in yours. Croissants are also called *brioche*, *briosca* and *cornetti*; they come *con marmellata* which almost
always means apricot jam, or *con crema*, with a custard filling. Whole-
wheat croissants with blueberry filling, flaky almond pastries and *krapfen*
– deep-fried puffs of dough filled with jam or cream – are other popular
choices in pastry shops and bars. Hot tea, hot chocolate and sometimes

fruit juices are available. If you do not see fresh oranges and a juicer you may well get a bottle or can of juice. Standing up at the bar is universally the least expensive way to have breakfast. Extra charges are usually added if you sit at a table and/or are served by a waiter.

Late Morning and Lunch

One of the best things about eating in Venice is *cichetti*. These bites of food, ranging from a simple chunk of salami to fried rice balls stuffed with seafood, are served up in *osterie* and bars all over town. *Cichetti* are popular both at lunch and right before dinner. As there are so many places to eat *cichetti*, many Venetians make them their lunch and dinner, easily filling their stomachs and visiting with friends at the same time. To eat *cichetti*, find one of the recommendations here, or simply walk into a place full of people standing and eating. Point at the items you want, order an *ombra* to wash it all down with, and when you are done pay and go to the next stop. You are on the honor system in Venice, but don't think you can walk out without paying, as there will be no taxicab in which to make a fast getaway.

Also popular at lunch are *tramezzini* and *panini*, available at virtually every bar in Venice. *Tramezzini* are triangle-shaped sandwiches with all kinds of fillings, such as prosciutto, tuna, or shrimp. Slathered with a good dose of mayonnaise, they are very addicting. *Panini* are rolls stuffed with variations of meats, cheese and vegetables. These are often piled on trays in the window or at the counter. In a good bar the *panini* move fast so you do not need to worry about getting yesterday's food.

Pizza and *calzone* are also popular choices for lunch. You can sit down and have an individual sized pizza served to you or eat a slice on the fly. Some bars offer a small spread of *cichetti*, pizza, pasta, and salads. If you are at a bar, and they have a big, full-color, glossy menu full of hot dishes, beware, as these are frozen entrees, not fresh food. This is not to say they won't taste good, but you can do better. If you want hot dishes for lunch, go to a trattoria or ristorante and sit down at a table. A plate of pasta, a salad, and water or wine makes a fine lunch; add another course if you'd rather nap after lunch than sightsee. In most restaurants it is perfectly fine to order at least one dish such as dessert *"uno per due,"* one portion for two people.

Don't forget you can order wine by the *mezzo* (half) or *quarto* (quarter) liter. It is usually easier to be served in a restaurant without a reservation at lunchtime than in the evening, but very popular places fill up quickly so if you are determined to have lunch in a particular place, do make a reservation.

In the late afternoon and evening in Venice, you will see the locals drinking pinkish-red beverages – these are Spritz. Spritz are made with white wine, a shot of either Aperol or Campari and a splash of soda, garnished with either an olive or a slice of lemon. A Venetian institution, you should try one at least once. Try ordering a *Spritz con Aperol*, which has a sweeter flavor, or a *Spritz con Campari* which is more bitter. Wine and beer are also consumed during the cocktail hour, along with lots of

Late Afternoon into Evening

cichetti. You might wonder how anyone could fit dinner in after all those *cichetti*, but it has been done.

Pizza is very popular and there are quite a few great pizzerias in Venice. Seafood and risotto are specialties of the Veneto and are on almost every restaurant menu. Wine or beer and water are usually drunk with a meal, and after dinner, you might enjoy a *sgroppino*, a delicious after-dinner drink made from vodka, Prosecco, and lemon sorbet.

Lots of Venetians stop for a gelato on their way home at night. There are fewer *gelaterie* open in the winter than in spring and summer, but with a little persistence you can find open places all year round. Do look for place with *"artigiano"* or homemade gelato and not prepacked products.

If you want to eat in a particular restaurant or even most trattorias on a given night, it is a good idea to make reservations. The concierge at your hotel can do this for you, or you can telephone on your own. Most places have someone who speaks some English answering the phone. You can also stop in, check out the menu and the ambience and then make reservations for that evening or for a future night. It is very difficult to have dinner earlier than 7:30; if you plan to go to a concert and need to eat early, have a big lunch and then have *cichetti* for dinner.

Sometimes you want to make a meal out of pizza, *panini*, *cichetti* or even gelato. Sometimes you want to go into a nicer restaurant, sit at a table, and be served several courses. Even in the most elegant restaurant it is not

necessary to have every course, and sharing an appetizer or dessert
is not usually a problem either.

Of course, you can always go for it all; you will probably be doing
enough walking to work off a few feasts. You can begin with an antipasto,
follow with a *primo piatto*, then a *secondo* and finally the *dolce*. Your
secondo or main course can be accompanied by one or more *contorni*
– side dishes. Usually you get your main dish with little more than a
garnish on the plate; you order everything else separately. Of course if
you have had a pasta before the meal, you might be quite happy to skip
the *contorni* and follow your entree with a salad or even skip to dessert.

In addition to a Spritz or cocktail before dinner and wine with it, you
might try a *digestivo* – an after-dinner drink following or instead of your
dessert. Coffee – almost always an espresso – is usually served as a separate course after the *dolce*. Remember you don't have to worry about
drinking and driving in Venice, but you do have to be able to walk home
or at least to the nearest vaporetto, preferably without falling into a canal.

Antipasti (appetizers)

Prosciutto e melone (ham and melon) is a safe and familiar appetizer,
and it is as readily available in Venice as it is all over Italy. Among the
most popular appetizers are *gransèola* (spider crab), *sarde in saòr* (fresh
sardines in a sweet and sour marinade), *molecche* (soft crabs), *baccalà
mantecà* (salted cod whipped with garlic flavored oil and parsley until it
is light and creamy), *schie* (tiny brown shrimp), *carpaccio* of meat or fish,
and/or an assortment of smoked fish or meats. If you are eating at an

osteria that serves *cichetti*, you can ask for a mixed plate of vegetable or seafood *cichetti* to start your meal. This is a wonderful way to sample the best *cichetti* of the house.

Primo Piatto (First course)

Primi piatti include soups, pastas and risottos. *Pasta e fagioli*, one of the true Venetian dishes, is a thick and hearty soup combining beans and pasta in a broth, which can be fish or meat based. It will turn up on almost every menu from the humblest trattoria to the more elegant ristorante, and it will never be exactly the same. Thicker, thinner, more beans, more pasta, each version will reflect the chef's interpretation of this classic soup. Just about every menu will also offer a thick and hearty vegetable soup, especially in winter. A seafood risotto is an elegant and traditional *primo* as is a risotto *primavera* – one made with fresh vegetables. *Risi e Bisi* – rice and peas cooked in a mixture somewhere between a soup and a risotto is another Venetian classic. *Bigoli in salsa* – a thick whole-wheat pasta in a sauce of onions and anchovies is a very traditional dish as is *spaghetti con seppie in nero* – spaghetti made black with cuttlefish ink. Almost any pasta *con frutti di mare* (with mixed seafood) will be outstanding in Venice as will any pasta with a specific seafood such as *penne con tonno* (with tuna) or *tagliatelle con granchio* (with crab). Diners who don't eat fish can usually find a Bolognese sauce or a simple *sugo di pomidoro* (tomato sauce) to sauce their pasta.

Secondo Piatto (Second course)

Unless you are a vegetarian, the *secondo* is when you make your big *pesce* (fish), or *carne* (meat) decision. Contrary to some rumors it is possible to order meat in Venetian restaurants. In fact, one of the most famous Venetian dishes is *fegato alla Veneziana* – calves' liver Venetian style. Even liver haters have been known to love this dish in which the meat is sliced into long, tendon-free slivers and cooked quickly and gently with onions in a little oil before being kissed with a sprinkling of parsley. As with *pasta e fagioli, fegato alla Veneziana* will vary slightly from place to place; more onions, no parsley, a dash of wine or vinegar – each dish represents a chef's vision of a true classic.

Veal will also turn up on most menus; a grilled veal chop, or a grilled pork chop, is a good bet in most trattorias, especially for the less adventurous eaters. A veal cutlet Milanese style – pounded, breaded and sautéed – is another good choice. In some versions, lovely fresh arugula is piled on top of your crisp cutlet.

Chicken is not often served in restaurants in Venice. Chicken cacciatore and chicken curry are more easily found than a basic roast chicken which is only occasionally seen on a trattoria menu. Duck and pheasant are more popular. Though many places offer *bistecca alla Fiorentina*, the steak is nothing like steak in Florence. Better choices for steak lovers would be the sliced filets often served with arugula, shavings of Parmigiano and balsamic vinegar, or a *costata* - rib steak. If the menu says it is sold by the *etto* the price will be based on the size of the steak. Braised beef dishes, beef stews and boiled beef are available especially in winter. Lamb is most often seen as "costolette" chops. They are generally cut more thinly than American chops but are very good especially when served with a wine or Balsamic sauce.

While a *bollito misto* in Milan or Bologna will mean a plate of assorted boiled meats, in Venice it is an assortment of steamed or boiled fish and shellfish. Even better than *bollito misto* is *fritto misto* – all sorts of sea creatures and vegetables batter-dipped and fried and piled to an alarming height on your plate.

If you are not up for a stack of sea critters, try a grilled fish. *Branzino* (Adriatic sea bass) is firm and white with a delicate flavor; it needs no more than a brush of olive oil and a dusting of parsley. *Rombo* (turbot) is often served with a coating of translucent potato slices. *Triglie* (red mullet) is a gorgeous pink fish that tastes even better than it looks; it is often served with *salsa di agrumi* (citrus sauce). *Orata* (gilthead) is another popular Adriatic fish, but be forewarned: an *orata* is small and will be served whole on your plate for you to bone yourself. *Branzino* and *rombo* will be presented to you whole and then whisked back to the kitchen or a side table where your waiter will bone it for you. A mixed seafood grill will include several of the above, a piece of sole or salmon and some scampi charred from the grill and bursting with smoky goodness.

Patate fritte (French fries) are available almost everywhere; other potato side dishes may be boiled potatoes, oven roasted potatoes, and pureed potatoes. Rice and pasta are eaten as the *primo piatto*, although they may be ordered as a *secondo*. Many places offer mixed grilled vegetables, which change seasonally; grilled radicchio and spinach are other popular *contorni*. Asparagus in season is magnificent and sometimes, large platters of them are served as either a *contorno* or a separate course. Do check the price on anything not listed on the menu to avoid surprises.

Salads are normally served after your *secondo* to cleanse the palate
for the *dolce*, but you may order a salad as an antipasto if you desire.
Insalata misto is mixed fresh vegetables usually topped with a generous
sprinkling of shredded carrots. *Insalata verde* is a plate of mixed greens.
Invariably, you will be served cruets of vinegar, olive oil, a shaker of salt
and sometimes a pepper mill. Your server will happily mix your dressing
for you, but it is easily done on your own – add a little oil, some salt
and pepper, and toss, then add the vinegar to taste and toss. *Balsamico*
(balsamic vinegar) is offered in some places; if you like it, and it is not
offered, request it.

Pane (bread) varies tremendously in Venice from wonderful crusty rolls
and slices of white or whole-wheat bread to rather dry hard tasteless
offerings. Butter is rarely served, but will be produced on request. Those
little dishes of seasoned olive oil so popular in Italian restaurants abroad
are virtually unheard of in Venice and the rest of Italy, for that matter,
although occasionally a cruet or bottle of olive oil is on the table to
be used as a garnish for your fish or meat.

Dolce are "sweets" - dessert - and can range from commercially produced
items to fruit and cheese to over-the-top homemade delights. Dessert
wines are also widely available, and *sgroppino* is another good way to
end a meal.

Smile and be happy. You are in Venice.

*THE*Restaurants OF *Venice*

There are six *sestiere* (districts) in Venice, and the listings are organized as such. San Marco, Castello, and Cannaregio are on the east side of the Grand Canal, and Santa Croce, San Polo, and Dorsoduro are on the west. Venetian addresses list the *sestiere*, and the number (such as Cannaregio, 653) with not much rhyme or reason to the numbering. Our listings have the name of the calle (street) and address number, with the *sestiere* listed on each page. We have also tried to give good walking instructions from the nearest vaporetto stop or landmark and you can get a basic idea of location in the maps at the back of this book. **Please do yourself a favor and invest in a good map before you get to Venice** – a company called Streetwise has a thorough and easy-to-read folding laminated map. All over Venice, yellow signs point the way to San Marco, Rialto, Accademia, Ferrovia (train station) and Piazzale Roma. These signs will help you navigate Venice and when needed we have included them in our walking instructions. Navigate from campo to campo and when in doubt, follow a Venetian.

Le Bistrot de Venise | www.bistrotdevenise.com

Calle dei Fabbri 4685 | Tel: 041-523-6651 | Fax: 041-520-2224

Very expensive | *Credit Cards* - *yes* | *Vaporetto* - *San Marco, Rialto*

Open: *Daily, 9:00 a.m. -1:00 a.m.*
Reservations: *recommended*

To get there: From Piazza San Marco, walk under the Sottoportego Dai, continue on Calle dei Fabbri, the restaurant will be on your right. From Rialto, walk down Riva del Carbon to Calle Bembo, continue on Calle dei Fabbri, the restaurant will be on your left.

Le Bistrot de Venise bills itself as an Arts Restaurant and Wine Bar, and has been known in the past for a fascinating menu with recreations of classical and historic Venetian dishes from the 14th & 15th centuries, a fantastic wine list, and non-Bistro prices. For the past ten years, the owners have been sponsoring regular poetry readings and literary discussions as well as art exhibits and wine tastings. An enoteca area is available during lunch with light and inexpensive suggestions for typical Venetian dishes, as well as a selection of Italian wines and *cichetti*. Outdoor dining is offered from April through October.

You will not encounter these recreations of historic dishes anywhere else and they are excellent. You might begin your meal with *Scampi in Saòr all Antica Agrodolci*, a recipe from an anonymous 14th century Venetian cook that combines scampi with sweet and sour stewed onions, almonds, Turkish grapes and spices. Paté lovers might enjoy *Fegato Grasso 'Oca au Torchon*, which is a parfait made from goose foie gras accompanied by a clove scented almond mousse and homemade chocolate bread. There is also an antipasto of four different types of fish, which vary according to the season and the fish market. *Bigoli alla Astice e Botolete*, a Venetian pasta specialty - spaghetti with lobster and tiny whole artichokes - is just one of the many pasta offerings. Traditionalists can enjoy the classic *Risi e Bisi*, based on a 15th century recipe; it is a risotto made with fresh peas, bacon and black pepper, and was originally created for a Doge so he could savor the first peas of spring on San Marco Day as was his privilege. For your *secondo* you can try wonderfully rare and juicy lamb with an herbal sauce, or from the historical menu, a 14th century recipe for *fileto de porca in savira aranzato* - filet of pork in orange and red wine sauce topped with small slices of sweet and tangy blood oranges. Other menu offerings include chicken with prunes, almonds, almond milk and spices or *branzino* in a ginger and saffron sauce which can be traced to the 15th century. Entrees are somewhat randomly accompanied by rice or potatoes, which can also be ordered as sides as can salads and grilled vegetables.

The wine list is superb. The Loredan Gasparini Capo di Stato is expensive and worth every penny. The dessert wines are magnificent. A Sauternes, Chateau Guiteronde de Hayot is like drinking Mel Torme's voice, and there are some really special aged Grappas, such as the Grappa Storica Domenis - Antica Distilleria Domenis Cividale del Fruili. A 1995 Vin

Santo Toscana - Vittorio Innocente del Montefollonico is an extraordinary example of that wine.

If you don't want to drink your dessert, the edible desserts are pretty spectacular; ginger cream with apple compote and crunchy rosemary brittle, or a modern version of a 15th century pumpkin cake with candied citron and almond cream are two of the many luscious treats on the menu. Some nights the waiter brings a complimentary digestive; on others the bill is accompanied by a treat, some crisp but sweet orange slices dipped in chocolate or tiny cups of warm liquid chocolate topped with whipped cream. Despite a hefty price tag, Le Bistrot de Venise offers a unique and memorable dining experience.

Vino Vino | www.anticomartini.com/vinovino.htm
Calle delle Veste 2007A | Tel: 041-241-7688

Inexpensive - moderate | *Credit Cards -* yes | *Vaporetto -* Vallaresso

Open: W-M, 10:30 a.m. to 11:30 p.m.
Reservations: not accepted

To get there: From the vaporetto stop, walk up Vallaresso, make a left on San Moise, continue on Calle Larga 22 Marzo, right on Calle del Sartor da Veste. The restaurant will be on your left.

Walk into the modernistic front room of Vino Vino, nod hello to the three or four gondoliers hanging out at the table next to the door, then check out the case of food in front of you. Order whatever items look most delectable, a bottle of wine from the extensive list, and move into the other room to wait for your selections to be served by the efficient, English speaking staff. The food is prepared next door at Vino Vino's sister restaurant, Antico Martini, and is served at a fraction of the price you would pay there.

Daily selections generally include a meat dish, a chicken dish, a couple of pastas, a lasagna, a rice dish, and several vegetable side dishes. The lasagna always stands out, and Vino Vino's artichoke version is particularly hard to beat. Veal scallopini is tender and fresh despite being reheated prior to being served, with a lemony sauce so good you'll want to use your bread to mop it all up. Roast chicken, in a town of notoriously bad chicken, is done simply and effectively and goes well with some of the rich vegetable side dishes. The vegetables offered might include asparagus wrapped in thin layers of prosciutto and grilled, fava beans drenched in olive oil, finely sliced onion and parsley, or broiled tomatoes with anchovy accented bread crumbs.

The wine list shines – with over 500 selections, you are sure to find something you like by the bottle, or simply choose one of the many selections offered by the glass. Wrap up the evening with a slice of hand-made torte and a glass of vin santo, and you'll leave Vino Vino happy.

Taverna La Fenice | www.tavernalafenice.it
Campo San Fantin 1939 | Tel: 041-522-3856 | Fax: 041-523-7866

Expensive | **Credit Cards -** *yes* | **Vaporetto -** *S. Maria d. Giglio*

Open: *M - Sat, dinner*
Reservations: *recommended*

To get there: The restaurant is towards the back of the La Fenice Theater and Campo San Fantin. There is another restaurant nearby with a similar name – make sure the address is right.

This classic Venetian restaurant had to close for months because of the work being done on the La Fenice opera house, and they used the time to spruce up the restaurant. The turn of the century elegance is still very much a part of the ambience, but everything looks a bit brighter and fresher than in the years immediately following the tragic fire at the opera house in whose shadow the restaurant stands. In winter it is particularly pleasant to be seated in one of the small cozy nooks while in summer seats near the windows or in the small campo in front of the building might be preferable.

La Fenice offers complimentary Prosecco, and the wine is excellent and properly chilled. The English speaking waiters are both friendly and professional. La Fenice is the sort of place in which you know the prosciutto will be delicate and pink, the melon at the peak of perfection, the fish the freshest obtainable, and the pasta cooked *al dente* and tossed with a mouthwatering sauce; however, it is in the area of risottos that La Fenice shines the brightest. Several risottos are listed on the menu and you cannot go wrong with any of them. *Risotto con funghi* is earthy and rich while *risotto primavera* sparkles with bright vegetable flavors. A more unusual risotto is made with *gò* and *beverasse*, a type of clam. *Gò* or *goby* is a mild white fish with a delicate flavor and firm texture that makes it perfect for a risotto. The clams add a pleasantly saline bite to the dish. La Fenice's version of *fegato alla Veneziana* ranks with the best of the best; in fact it could be the standard for this dish. The veal liver is tender, moist and still rosy; the onions are mild and not a bit greasy and the balance of the two is perfect. Lamb chops are served nicely pink and are not too fatty, but the sauce with *finferli* mushrooms can be a little salty for some palates. All the classics can be found among the fish dishes, with the *San Pietro* receiving star treatment. *Branzino* is often available in more than one style. It might be accompanied by *radicchio de Treviso* or with zucchini blossoms and an assortment of vegetables.

Profiteroles, covered with chocolate and whipped cream and studded with a chocolate starburst come with a small chocolate sign saying Taverna La Fenice and, in a bit of whimsy presentation, a nonexistent fork outlined in cocoa powder on the white plate. The *sorbetto*, the Taverna's version of *sgroppino*, is very lemony and the perfect conclusion to a big meal. The cheese platter is exceptional in both quality and variety. *Tiramisù*, fruit tarts and gelato are among the other dessert choices.

The second time we went to Le Bistro de Venise we nearly walked right by it because it was so dark. We knew we had reservations, and could not imagine why they would be closed, but upon closer examination, we discovered their lights were out. The kitchen was up and running, but we had to choose between dining by candlelight or eating elsewhere. Since we had really enjoyed our first dinner there, a candlelight supper seemed a good option. We were ushered in past the bar to the no smoking area and seated in a row of small tables, each with a lighted candle on it. It was a little tricky to read the menu in the dim light but somehow it seemed appropriate for a place that specialized in both classical and historic Venetian cuisine. It did not take long to appreciate the magical effect candlelight had on those of a certain age and those who were significantly younger. While we were eating, others came in; those who did not have candles on their tables shared with neighbors. The food was as good as on our first visit, but the conversational hum seemed softer and mellower. Towards the end of our meal, the lights came on. There was a moment of silence, and then a disappointed sounding collective "Aww!" "Turn the lights off again!" someone said; his suggestion was received with applause. – *R.E.*

Corte Sconta
Calle del Pestrin 3886 | Tel: 041-522-7024 | Fax: 041-522-7513

Expensive - very expensive | **Credit Cards:** yes | **Vaporetto:** Arsenale

Open: T - Sat, lunch and dinner
Reservations: strongly recommended

To get there: From the Riva degli Schiavoni along the lagoon, take the Calle d. Forno to Calle Pestrin.

Though Corte Sconta means "hidden courtyard" the restaurant itself is easier to find than its name might indicate. There is no printed menu, but the owner and waiters all speak excellent English and are happy to explain the dishes.

Corte Sconta is justly famous for their seafood antipasto which is several courses consisting of whatever is freshest and best in the market that day. You are greatly encouraged to order this, and if you have the appetite and pocketbook for it, you should indulge yourself. You might find fresh salmon marinated in lemon juice and Tuscan olive oil with arugula and pomegranates; a mildly spiced spider crab pâté; spider crab and crab roe in the shell with oil, lemon and black pepper; and/or baby shrimp with grilled slices of both yellow and white polenta. Everything is perfectly cooked and as fresh as can be. Possibly the most famous single item in the antipasto is the ginger clams. These are tiny *vongole veraci* cooked with parsley, garlic, oil and ginger. If you don't want the works you can order any of the items individually; do let the owner recite all the possibilities to you. Though the antipasto is the more unusual and interesting way to begin a meal, you can also start with a pasta. A good choice, if available, is *tagliolini* with fresh tuna. You may order an individual fish such as grilled *branzino* or a platter of mixed grilled or fried fish. The platter of grilled fish is likely to include *rombo*, sole, *coda di rospo, branzino* and scampi which are grilled in their shells until they are lightly charred. *Contorni* include various types of potatoes, grilled radicchio and a platter of fresh grilled vegetables.

The house wine is a very drinkable still Prosecco. Lemon sorbet with a shot of vodka is a light *dolce* after a full meal. For those who would like to splurge on dessert, there is *zabaglione*, which is like a thick, creamy Marsala, or a lovely and generous assortment of cookies.

Corte Sconta is a seafood-only restaurant that has excellent food, but they do have a tendency to coax guests into ordering very large, and very expensive meals. If you stand firm and order only as much as you are comfortable eating, it will not in the least affect the quality of your meal.

Alla Strega
Barbaria d. Tole 6418 | Tel: 041-528-6497

Inexpensive | *Credit Cards:* no | *Vaporetto:* Ospedale

Open: T - Sun lunch and dinner
Reservations: not needed

To get there: From the front of Church of S.S. Giovanni & Paolo, walk through the Campo with the church on your left. Continue down Barbaria d. Tole, the restaurant will be on your right. A sign with a witch riding her broomstick is above the door.

This great pizzeria is extremely popular with the locals both to eat in and to take out. You won't get anything but pizza, entrée salads, and French fries here, but it would be impossible for anyone save a die-hard pizza hater not to find something on the menu at Alla Strega. They offer pizza with no cheese, pizza with no sauce, pizza with only sauce, or only cheese. Try the *Diavolo*, covered with spicy sausage and gorgonzola, or the *Halloween*, topped with pumpkin and tiny crumbs of biscotti, or ricotta and spinach with a fried egg in the middle. Salads are ample and interesting and come with an oil and salt covered pizza bread hot from the oven. Desserts are purchased off-site and the wine is so-so; beer, water, or soda are better bets.

Strega means witch and the fitting décor is Halloween-themed year around, the music is generally Bob Marley or Lenny Kravitz, and the staff is ready to get out of there at midnight or earlier. For a true slice of Venetian life, sit out on the patio under vine-topped lattices in the summer and listen to Venetian teenagers argue with their parents.

Alla Rivetta
Salizzada San Provolo 4625 | Tel: 041-528-7302

Moderate | *Credit Cards:* yes | *Vaporetto:* San Zaccaria

Open: T - Sun, 11 a.m. - 11 p.m.
Reservations: recommended

To get there: From Piazza San Marco, walk to the left of the Basilica, make a right at the canal, cross over the bridge. Keep going until you get to the next bridge – the restaurant is on the right before you cross the bridge.

Tucked in a corner almost under the Ponte San Provolo, Alla Rivetta is no newcomer to the Venice scene. It may be hard to believe that this bright and crowded trattoria smack dab in the middle of tourist mania has great food at reasonable prices, but indeed it does. The front room has long tables at which people are seated with groups overlapping as space allows; a small back room has more traditional seating of tables of four. If you don't have a reservation, expect to wait, but things move quickly here, and you never feel rushed while dining.

The extensive menu offers a large variety of meat and fish dishes. You can begin with the ever-popular prosciutto, an assortment of salamis, a vegetable antipasto, or perhaps just the eggplant topped with anchovy and cheese. On a cold night, you might try one of several soups including *tortellini in brodo*. Spaghetti with *vongole veraci* is a better than average version of this classic dish with a nice balance of flavors; kick it up a notch by drizzling some spicy olive oil over your pasta. Lasagna with mushrooms and *speck* (ham) is so rich and creamy that the waiter insists it will make a full meal, and he is right. Fried shrimp and calamari is a nice sized serving, crisp and not greasy, while an order of *scampi alla griglia* is wonderfully smoky with the slightly charred taste enhancing the scampi's own flavor. There are several beef and veal dishes listed as well as roast chicken and pork chops. There is also a wide choice of *contorni*. Desserts are pretty standard, and the *tiramisù*, at least, is nothing special, but there are some good grappas and a wonderful almond flavored sweet wine available if you ask.

The waiters are all friendly and helpful. Alla Rivetta is not for those bothered by noise, nor would it be a good choice for anyone suffering from claustrophobia, but there is something for everyone on the menu, and it gives great value for your Euro.

Alle Testiere
Calle del Mondo Novo 5801 | Tel & Fax: 041-522-7220

Expensive | *Credit Cards:* yes | *Vaporetto:* Rialto

Open: T - Sat, lunch and dinner
Reservations: essential

To get there: From Campo Santa Maria Formosa, walk towards Rialto down Calle Mondo Nuovo. The restaurant will be on your left.

This tiny but justifiably popular seafood-only restaurant offers only two seatings a night - one at 7:00 p.m. and one at 9:30 p.m. and since no more than 24 people are served at a time, reservations and promptness are both important. Alle Testiere means "at the headboards," and there are old wooden headboards making up part of the bar, and old wrought iron headboards hanging on the walls.

The owner recites the menu of the day, and at the back of the wine list there is a price list for most of the standard dishes so you can get an idea of what your meal will cost. The owner and most of the friendly and ef-ficient staff speak at least some English.

Canestrelli - tiny scallops grilled with balsamic vinegar - are an excel-lent choice among the antipasti. Oysters grilled with fennel are another wonderful antipasto with little bits of fennel fronds, salad greens, a bit of tomato and something with a touch of heat bringing out the anise taste of the fennel which goes well with the briny oysters.

A grilled fish platter for two will be boned and divided for you if you wish. A typical platter might include a giant prawn with the head still attached and the tail loosened and resting in its shell. There might also be a tender and delicate baby squid - just the perfect size to pop right in your mouth, a piece of monk fish that is tender and mild tasting without being bland, or a filet of angler fish. Everything is impeccably fresh and prepared with loving care.

The basket of breads, rolls and breadsticks contains an interesting and tasty assortment. The house wine, which can be ordered in a full, *mezzo* or even a quarter carafe, is unusually good. Alle Testiere is also known for their small but carefully chosen list of wines by the bottle.

There is an awesome list of desserts, among them a chestnut mousse and a cherry cake that are definitely not the typical Venetian restaurant *dolce*. There are some wonderful cheeses offered, and for those preferring to sip their dessert, a *passito* of Sauvignon Blanc is a lovely way to end a meal.

This delightful restaurant is a semi-hidden treasure. One has to wonder if all those vague slightly misleading directions to this gem are an accident, or if fans are trying to keep the place to themselves. Don't let them.

Osteria Da Alberto
Calle Giacinto Gallina 5401 | Tel: 041-523-8153

Moderate | *Credit Cards:* yes | *Vaporetto:* Fondamenta Nove, Rialto

Open: M - Sat, Lunch and dinner
Reservations: essential for dinner, recommended for lunch

To get there: From the Chiesa d. Miracoli walk towards the Chiesa S.S. Giovanni & Paolo. The restaurant will be on your right.

This bustling osteria gets absolutely packed at lunchtime and before dinner when it is a stop for Venetians in the neighborhood for *cichetti* and conversation. Behind the 4' X 4' area where fifteen people stand munching and drinking, there are two small, casual dining rooms. It is here that some of the best food in Venice is served up at a fraction of the price you'll pay in some tourist joints right up the street.

Ignore the printed-in-four-languages menu. Instead, concentrate on what is displayed on the *cichetti* bar and the daily specials, posted in the window and recited tableside by one of the hip and super-friendly staff. The specials change every couple of days and are the same price for lunch and dinner. Generally, one to two pastas, a risotto, a fish entree, and a meat entree are offered. To start, share a plate of vegetable or seafood *cichetti*, and then depending on the size of your appetite, go from there. Pasta is often topped with a fish sauce, such as a fantastic tuna and tomato version that envelopes the senses, or scampi and radicchio. Risotto is slightly more cooked than at other Venetian restaurants, and must be ordered for two. Da Alberto does great things with radicchio, and their risotto with radicchio and gorgonzola is fantastic, the bitter vegetable and the pungent cheese being perfect partners here. Fish is very fresh and very basic, generally grilled and served whole, on your plate. The daily meat is usually a filet of beef and is always tender and flavorful and often comes with a delicious, aromatic sauce, such as tomatoes and zucchini stewed in wine, or a light gorgonzola sauce. Green salads are your basic arugula with some grated carrot, as seems to be the Venetian way.

House wine is good and very reasonable, and a selection of bottled wine is available. Desserts are purchased off-site; enjoy a plate of local cheeses with the last of your wine or stop for gelato on your way home.

Fiaschetteria Toscana | Tel : 041-528-5281
Salizzada San Giovanni Crisostomo 5719 | Fax: 041-528-5521

Expensive | *Credit Cards:* yes | *Vaporetto:* Rialto

Open: W-M, Lunch and dinner
Reservations: essential

To get there: From Rialto, walk left through Campo San Bartolomeo, pass the Post Office on your left and Bacaro Jazz on your right. Continue on Salizzada San Giovanni Crisostomo. The restaurant will be on your left.

This well-known and very popular restaurant is recommended but with a caveat: Do Not Sit Upstairs. Downstairs you will find superb food with proper service; up the steep and slippery stairs where they seat larger groups and overflow customers, you will find the same good food but also indifferent, sloppy service.

To start your meal, a plate of fresh, sweet oysters have just enough brininess to prove they come from the sea. Accompanied by a glass of chilled Prosecco, they cannot be topped as a first course. Foie gras with *picolit*, a rare, sweet wine from Friuli, is an expensive and classic combination. For the *primi*, spaghetti with *vongole veraci* is a good opener, especially if you like garlic. The *pasta e fagioli* is an outstanding version of this hearty bean soup. The *gnocchetti* with shrimp is also delicious. Fiaschetteria Toscana is a member of the Buon Ricordo Association; this means they have a featured dish which comes on a commemorative plate that you get to keep. The Buon Ricordo plate, *La Serenissima*, is a generous tangle of lightly battered and fried seafood and vegetables. Don't be shy about asking for your plate, a busy waiter might forget. For those who are not feeling peckish, the grilled *Pesce San Pietro* is a light and simple choice. Lamb chops are tender and juicy and are accompanied by pureed potatoes and perfectly cooked fresh spinach. *Fegato alla Veneziana* is hearty and satisfying. *Contorni* of steamed or grilled vegetables are usually available, and might include string beans, carrots, zucchini, fennel and cauliflower. The very fine olive oil the waiter drizzles over the dish perks everything up.

The wine list is one of the best in Venice. The owner's wife is the pastry chef and if her *Chibousta* is on the menu, go for it. It is an almond cake topped with *zabaglione* and fresh raspberries surrounded by a bright red puddle of an incredibly intense raspberry sauce. Apple cake with ice cream or cake with whipped cream filling accompanied by a lovely puddle of strawberry sauce are both good choices. For a pricey splurge, have the *zabaglione*. It is superbly made with an incredible texture. Eating a cloud permeated by the flavor of marsala is a wonderful end to a meal.

Casa Mia
Calle dell'Oca 4430 | Tel: 041-528-5590

***Inexpensive - Moderate** | **Credit Cards:** yes | **Vaporetto:** Ca' D'Oro, Rialto*

***Open:** W-M, lunch and dinner*
***Reservations:** accepted*

To get there: From Campo Santi Apostoli at the foot of Strada Nova, find Calle dell'Oca to the left of the church. The restaurant will be on your right.

This homey, comfortable restaurant has an engaging pizza chef, incredible pizza and very slow service. Walk in and try to flag someone down to get you a table, or if you are female, get the pizza chef's attention – he has a soft spot for women and usually seats them immediately. If you are lucky, the pizza chef will seat you right in front of him where you can watch him make one delicious pizza after another.

A pizza with *salame nostrano* and *radicchio de Treviso* is an excellent choice, as is the asparagus and porcini mushroom. A kitchen in the back of the house offers a variety of pastas and main courses that are as popular with the Venetian clientele as the pizzas are with the tourists. Desserts are commercially produced.

Alla Vecia Cavana
Rio Terà SS Apostoli 4624 | Tel & Fax 041-528-7106

Moderate – Expensive | *Credit Cards:* yes | *Vaporetto:* Ca' D'Oro, Rialto

Open: T - Sun, lunch and dinner
Reservations: recommended

To get there: from Campo Santi Apostoli at the foot of Strada Nova, walk with the church on your right to Salizzada d. Pistor. Make a right on Rio Terra dei Franceschi to Rio Terà SS. Apostoli.

Alla Vecia Cavana, once Il Sole Sulla Vecia Cavana, recently changed hands and is now owned by the same family that owns Al Pantalon in Dorsoduro and Alla Patatina in San Polo. It is not as glamorous as it was when it was owned by the Il Sole group, but the service is much faster. The prices as well as the level of cooking have come down since our last visits, and the dining room is more boisterous.

Upon arrival, diners receive glasses of chilled Prosecco as well as along with a small dish of olive paté, which accompanies the bread basket. A house *amuse bouche* is also offered. On a recent night it was a gratineed oyster on the half shell resting on a bed of baby greens.

For prosciutto lovers, the *Artigianale* prosciutto from Oswald, in the Dolomites, is a must have because it is truly spectacular. In winter it is served with incredibly juicy and sweet cherry tomatoes, which make a brilliant partner for the ham. The *parmigiano* basket in which it is served is more of a cup than a woven basket and can be disappointingly dry and a little greasy.

The menu offers both meat and fish dishes and is decidedly less elegant than it used to be, but the *branzino* with its potato coating is delicious; though the potatoes are crunchy and crusty on top and tender under-neath, and the fish is tender and fresh, the portion of fish is too small. Among the other listings there are many tempting items, but several favor-ites from the Il Sole days have vanished. Among the *dolce*, the poached pear with gelato is a good choice; it is made to order and the ice cream which is encased in the pear melts endearingly into its flesh, which does make it difficult to share.

The house white wine, a Chardonnay, is an outstanding one, but the bread basket is nowhere near as interesting as it used to be. The wine list and wine service are more befitting a typical osteria than a ristorante. Despite basically very good food, and much prompter service, Alla Vecia Cavana has not completely jelled. It may be caught between what it was and what it will be. Time will tell, but it is still definitely worth a try.

Trattoria da Alvise
Fondamente Nove 5045 | Tel: 041-520-4185

Moderate | *Credit Cards:* yes | *Vaporetto:* Fondamenta Nove

Open: T -Sun, lunch and dinner
Reservations: accepted

To get there: From the Fondamente Nove vaporetto stop, facing the water, walk right a bit, the restaurant will be on your right.

This cheery pizzeria-trattoria on the Fondamente Nove offers spectacular views of the lagoon and the cemetary island of San Michele. In mild weather you can sit under an awning at tables right on the Fondamenta and watch the vaporettos and other boats crossing the sparkling water. Inside there are two rooms; the larger room with the bar offers the same spectacular view from almost every seat; the adjoining room is more limited in views but is pleasant and cheery. Da Alvise is definitely child-friendly, with a cheerful owner and a welcoming staff.

Begin your meal with any of the traditional antipasti, soups or pastas. *Spaghetti con vongole* is nicely done with fresh clams and a healthy amount of garlic and parsley. *Spaghetti Bolognese*, unaccountably, is meatless, but the tomato sauce is sprightly and delicious. Roast veal has an unusual but nicely done red wine sauce ladled carefully over tender slices of white meat. You can find all the traditional Venetian meat and fish dishes at Da Alvise. There is an extensive wine list and a good assortment of beers as well.

Iguana

Fondamenta Misercordia 2515 | Tel: 041-713561

Inexpensive - moderate | *Credit Cards* - *yes* | *Vaporetto* - *Ca' D'Oro*

Open: *T-Sat dinner; Sun, lunch and dinner, service until 11p.m.*
Reservations: *accepted and recommended for canal-side tables*

To get there: From Ca' D'Oro, make a left on Strada Nova to Campo San Felice. Make a right up Fondamenta Chiesa, continue on Fondamenta San Felice, left on Misercordia, the restaurant will be on your right.

Fondamenta Misercordia is a great street on which to eat. A number of restaurants with outside dining line the canal, and the choices are eclectic and more international than anywhere in Venice. One of the best choices here is Iguana, a funky, slightly grungy, completely cool place. Along with Paradiso Perduto up the street, this is where the hipsters of the neighborhood come for drinking, dinner and for the weekly live music they offer. This Mexican/Venetian hybrid has menus in English and in Italian. Try to get a copy of each as some of the best options are offered only on the Italian menu.

Start with an appetizer order of *salsa misto*, which includes a red salsa, guacamole, a white garlicky dip, and a tasty black bean dip. The chips contain enough oil to fill a deep fryer, but a bit of grappa after dinner cuts through it. Chicken enchiladas are layered like lasagna, and come from the kitchen bubbling hot and very rich. There is a decent quesadilla filled with chicken, shrimp, or beef, topped with guacamole. Skip the tacos, they don't have the concept down on that one yet. The salads are very good and come with a range of southwestern toppings such as red beans and corn and a ranch-style dressing which is a delight after the ubiquitous oil & vinegar on every other Venetian table. On the Italian menu only is a good, if a little bland, plate of fajitas.

A wide range of tequila is available and a selection of spiked coffee drinks is offered after dinner. A great place to go when you just can't face another pizza or want to hang out with the locals.

Vini da Gigio | www.vinidagigio.com
Fondamenta Chiesa 3628A Tel: 041-528-5140 Fax: 041-522-8597

Moderate - expensive | Credit Cards - no **| Vaporetto -** Ca' D' Oro

Open: W -Sun, lunch and dinner
Reservations: essential

From Ca' D' Oro, walk straight back to Strada Nova. Go left and cross over the first bridge. Make an immediate right so the Church of San Felice is on your left and the Rio di San Felice is on your right. The restaurant will be directly ahead of you just past the church.

Tucked just off Strada Nova with an unassuming entrance, Vini da Gigio is an outstanding restaurant that can be given top marks in every category. The food, wine list, service and ambience are all wonderful, and, all things considered, the prices are reasonable.

Those wanting to pack in a *primo, secondo* and *dolce* (which we highly recommend here) might start with a vegetable antipasto; a plate of very fresh, simply prepared vegetables such as sautéed spinach, steamed Brussels sprouts and grilled radicchio served with only a fruity olive oil as an accompaniment. Mixed fish plates are another option with a smoked fish plate featuring eel being one good choice. The *Misto Crudo*, a selection of raw fish, features whatever is freshest and best in the fish market that day as does the *Misto di Pesce*, which might include such goodies as *baccalà* fritters, *schie* and broiled scallops.

Primi include plump, light as a feather gnocchi with pesto and shrimp or fusilli with *radicchio de Treviso* and crunchy pancetta in winter, asparagus and tomato in the spring. Arugula stuffed ravioli come with a rich, sensual *taleggio* cheese sauce - called a *zabaglione* - that tastes so good you'll want to bathe in it.

Spaghetti with *caparozzoli* - the small clams also known as *vongole veraci* - is a classic Venetian dish done to perfection here. The *tagliolini* with crab is another classic, which offers no fancy sauces or flowery herbs - just perfectly cooked pasta and incredibly fresh crabmeat. The penne with Gorgonzola and pistachios is a rich and sensual pasta offering, while the rigatoni with duck sauce has lots of tasty bits of duck meat in a brown sauce which clings to the ridges of the pasta as well as hiding inside the little tubes.

Among the *secondi*, there is an exceptional *fegato alla Veneziana* that ranks with the best in Venice. Steak with red pepper sauce is superb and a great choice for red meat lovers. Duck "Burano" style is stewed and though the flavor is delicious it lacks the crispy skin that is obtained by roasting. *Osso buco* has a well-balanced, flavorful sauce, tender veal and a succulent marrow bone. The lamb is simply amazing. It has an encrusted exterior that is magical, and the meat itself is pink, delicate and incredibly juicy.

The breadbasket here contains lots of interesting treats and the wine list includes over a thousand bottles that are very well-priced. Le Due Terre Sacrisassi, which is a blend of Tocai and Ribolla from Mascarelli, is an incredible golden color, and the flavor is a perfect with most pastas. One of the great bargains on the wine list, a 1997 Villa Gemma Montepuliciano from Abruzzi would be another great choice. The 1995 Bertani Amarone della Valpollicella Classico is a huge wine with an incredible depth of flavor, and although pricey, it is a fraction of what it would cost outside of Italy.

Desserts come in for their share of raves too. The *tiramisù* is excellent as is a small round *torte di cioccolato*, which arrives on a plate decorated with warm chocolate. *Crème Catalan* is almost too rich and creamy. It is served in a special dish that has a little well for the custard with two delicate cookies on the edge of the custard, and the wide rim of the plate deliciously and beautifully decorated with powdered sugar, and swirls of other sweet treats - it would be worth ordering for the presentation alone. The star of the desserts is the heavenly Almond Crumby cake with *Sabaione (zabaglione.)* The cake itself is lovely, the *sabaione* perfection, and it is addictive. A Sardinian wine, Angiali da Isola de Nuraghi, is the perfect vino *dolce* with or in lieu of dessert.

Al Fontego dei Pescaori | Tel: 041-520-0538 Fax: 041-277-1716
Sottoportego del Tagiapiera 3711-3712

Moderate | *Credit Cards - yes* | *Vaporetto - Ca' D' Oro*

Open: T - Sun, lunch and dinner
Reservations: recommended

To get there: from Ca' D' Oro, walk to Strada Nova. Turn left, cross the first bridge, and make an immediate right. Go over the first bridge on your right; cross the Rio di San Felice and walk under the archways. The restaurant is just a few steps ahead on your right.

Pescaori means "fisherman" in Venetian and the owner has had a stall in the fish market for 25 years. The interior consists of two cheerful rooms decorated with paintings of Venice. The cool, lovely garden is covered by a large awning and there are stone boxes full of geraniums, climbing roses and greenery all around. It is quieter than the indoor rooms, and has a tranquil feel to it.

Diners are given complimentary glasses of Prosecco with their menus, which include both a tasting menu and a la carte offerings. Among the antipasto offerings are grilled scallops, which have been lightly dusted with cheese. Tuna tartare is more coarsely chopped than some versions, but is absolutely first rate in freshness and flavor and often comes presented on a plate "painted" with very old balsamic vinegar and garnished with a blueberry, a blackberry and a raspberry; an inspired combination.

Primi include a sensational *orecchiette* with seafood and white asparagus or *bigoli* with duck sauce. Try the *farfalle* with *frutti di mare* and rocket (arugula) sauce. The pasta is loaded with lots of little sea creatures - tiny clams, small but plump mussels, and bits of scallop, just to name a few – and topped with not much more than extra virgin olive oil and juices from the various bits of seafood. The rocket sauce - a gorgeous bright green puree of fresh arugula - drapes the edges of the dish. *Gnocchetti* with scallops and zucchini is another good starter with a lovely sauce including both the white and coral parts of the scallop chopped into a fine dice and highlighted with bits of bright green zucchini.

Among the *secondi*, the *Pesce San Pietro* with spinach is simple but excellent as is the *branzino*, which comes topped with its own wonderfully crisp and crunchy back skin and a delectable frizzle of zucchini. Tuna is served rare with only the outer edges cooked to whiteness and rests on an artichoke bottom topped with spinach and enlivened by a generous drizzle of aged *balsamico*. *Fegato alla Veneziana* is gristle free and is accompanied by superbly cooked onions, but the meat is in small pieces instead of the more traditional long, thin strips.

The tasting menu is very nicely presented; there is an assortment of antipasto, followed by two small servings of pasta, three small pieces of fish, and a small assortment of desserts. There are many gems on the wine list, and the house wine is excellent.

The house *tiramisù* is an excellent interpretation of what has become a dessert standard. There is also a warm chocolate cake, mascarpone cream, and crème brulee. An order of biscotti and *vino dolce* includes a plate with several small vanilla and chocolate almond butter cookies and a glass of *fragolino*, which is delightful, but there are even better treats on the wine list. In particular, a 2002 Franz Haas Moscato Rosa from the Alto Adige is not inexpensive, but it is extraordinary.

Most of the staff speak some English, and a few are fluent. Certainly the owner is very conscientious and very hands-on as well as being both affable and welcoming. He truly wants his customers to enjoy their meal. As a final treat, pretty little Murano glass candies are given to female diners when the *conto* is brought to the table.

Boccadoro
Campo Widman 5405A | Tel: 041-521-1021

Moderate | *Credit Cards* - *yes* | *Vaporetto* - *Rialto, Ca' D'Oro*

Open: T - Sun, lunch and dinner
Reservations: recommended

To get there: The restaurant is in Campiello Widman, near Chiesa S. Maria Miracoli.

Since our first edition, Boccadoro has changed hands. The new chef-owner, Luciano, is just as passionate about seafood as the previous chef was, and has expanded the dining room to accommodate more lucky diners.

We have learned from a regular that the restaurant does not have a freezer or a can opener, and that they make their pasta by hand every day. We believe it. The pasta here is stellar, and is always served with some sort of fish unless otherwise requested. Pasta made with *seppe* (cuttlefish) and topped with a delicate artichoke sauce is a delightful *primo*, as is a simple *Spaghetti alle Vongole*. Luciano is very creative, as his *Tagliatelle con Capesante e Fiori di Zucca* will attest. Pasta with scallops and squash flowers – it doesn't get much better than this.

Secondi include a selection of grilled and sauteéd fish dishes made up of whatever Luciano spots at the market that day. Try turbot with a sauce

of *radicchio di Treviso*, a piece of seared *tonno* topped with arugula
and baby tomatoes, or a *fritto misto* lightly battered and perfectly fried.
Boccadoro is not a place for diners who don't want seafood - there is no
meat on the menu, and though they will whip up a very nice hand-made
fettucini with tomato sauce, it will come at a fairly high price.

The housemade desserts are simple and well-made, and the wine list
has many nice bottlings that shine with fish dishes. Luciano is on hand,
greeting and seating people, and helping with the menu; it is clear that he
wants diners to enjoy themselves. He creates a feeling of well-being in
the room and after you eat his pasta, you'll share that feeling with him.

Da Fiore
Calle del Scaleter 2202 | Tel: 041-721-308 | Fax: 041-721-1343

Very Expensive | *Credit Cards* - *yes* | *Vaporetto* - *San Tomà, San Stae*

Open: *T - Sat, lunch and dinner*
Reservations: *essential - fax ahead*

**To get there: From San Stae, follow Salizzada San Stae and follow the
yellow signs to Rialto** – after a few twists and turns you will run smack
into it. From Campo San Polo, look towards Rialto with the church at your
back, and walk to the left. At the back of the campo you exit to the right
at Rio Terà San Antonio. Continue on Calle Bernardo and then on Calle
del Scaleter. The restaurant is just over the bridge on your left. It is a most
unassuming entrance; the glories are all inside.

It is a lovely thing when a place lives up to and possibly even exceeds its reputation. Because this absolute gem of a restaurant is not only excellent but small and extremely popular, reservations must be made well in advance. Its unprepossessing entrance leads into a small bar area from which one passes into a waiting room and finally the dining room. The decor is simplicity itself, but every detail is done well and done right. In the softly lit dining room, small bouquets of fresh flowers decorate every table; the napery is white and spotless; the glasses sparkle in the glow of the shaded candle on each table. The walls are covered with a woven straw fabric; the ceramic plates are a gentle brown and white pattern. A winning touch is a low stool next to each table at the place where the woman is seated; it is there to hold purses, cameras, guide books – whatever it would be inconvenient to have on the table or hanging from your chair. Brilliant! The service is impeccable but friendly.

The wine list is large and leather bound, the menu is small; four or five antipasti; two soups, two salads, four or five *primi* and four or five *secondi*. The menu is completely in Italian and usually only one will have prices. The staff is fluent in English and is more than willing to translate and explain. Your meal will begin with an introductory treat such as a small puddle of creamy white polenta next to a scattering of battered and fried baby shrimp and zucchini circles. An excellent first course is the *rossette scottato* – baby red mullet sautéed and served with sweet tart oranges and an arugula salad. Other choices might include scallops gratineed in their shells or a *fritto misto* of autumn vegetables.

An unusual pasta dish is the house special of spinach *pappardelle* with mussels and other mollusks.

The *rombo al forno* in a potato crust makes a superb *secondo*. It is a generous piece of fish boned by a master with an outer coating of thin, crisp potato slices. A bright green herbal infusion adds a splash of color to the plate and compliments the flavor of the fish. A filet of *branzino* with balsamic vinegar is presented as a round green disk; the fish has been wrapped in an edible leaf and then placed atop some gently cooked green apples. Soft shell crabs are crunchy and delicious; they are accompanied by rich creamy polenta and tangy crisp arugula. *Crema con zucchero flambé* (crème brulee) is an outstanding interpretation of a classic dessert. Green apple *sorbetto* with a perfume of grappa nestles in an ice flower topped with a fringe of green apple slices. Homemade vanilla ice cream comes with a pear poached in white wine and then coated in chocolate. A lighter dessert is a pineapple soup – a fantasy of fresh fruit floating in a chilled pineapple puree. A small plate of cookies appears with your coffee or with the *conto*.

Da Fiore is definitely expensive, and it is definitely worth it. Add this place to your list of romantic sites for special occasion dinners, and if your pocketbook allows it, add it to your list for the best of Venetian food.

Antico Dolo | www.anticodolo.it
Ruga Vecchio San Giovanni 778 | Tel: 041-522-6546

Moderate | *Credit Cards - yes* | *Vaporetto - San Silvestro*

Open: *T - Sun, lunch and dinner*
Reservations: *recommended*

To get there: From the Rialto Bridge, walk straight and make your first left. The restaurant will be on your right.

Squeeze past the tables in the narrow corridor, step up to the bar, order some wine and *cichetti* and settle in to wait for a table at this tiny, bustling trattoria. With seating for no more than thirty, and the kitchen tucked upstairs in the back, a trio of servers dips and dodges through eager patrons, delivering steaming plates with a flourish and a smile.

A good way to open a meal is with a huge platter of vegetable antipasto. Some are in the form of *crostini*, and others have sauces in contrasting colors; the selection changes on a daily and seasonal basis. Assorted appetizers can also be chosen from the display at the bar. The *risotto con verdure* takes 20 minutes to prepare, and is worth the wait. A small, gray heap in the middle of an enormous white plate, festooned with shredded carrots and bits of parsley, it is less than attractive in appearance, but is perfectly cooked and infused with the flavor of mushrooms and radicchio that give it such a funky color. A seafood risotto is also available. *Spaghetti neri*, colored with squid ink, is a popular pasta here, as is *spaghetti con frutti di mare*, with a generous helping of fresh, mixed seafood. Homemade gnocchi float in a sauce of olives, tomatoes and vegetables. Fish like *orata* and *branzino alla griglia* are very fresh, perfectly cooked and served whole but if you ask, the kitchen will bone the fish for you. The *tiramisù* is served as an individual portion in a deep bowl, and is much soupier than most, lusciously rich and wonderful. The *sgroppino* is also outstanding.

Trattoria San Tomà
Campo San Tomà 2864/A | Tel: 041-523-8819

Moderate | *Credit Cards* - yes | *Vaporetto* - San Tomà

Open: W - M, lunch and dinner
Reservations: accepted

To get there: The restaurant is in Campo San Tomà.

An Italian friend who prides himself on his ability to find the best pizza places got such good vibes from this place we agreed to try it. The Margherita - the standard test run for a pizza - is definitely better than average here; the Brie and arugula has enough greens on it to stock a salad bar for a week, plus a generous amount of bubbling Brie and the *vegetariano* has an amazing assortment of vegetables that changes with the seasons. Dozens of pizzas are offered, and special requests are accommodated.

A full menu is also available. *Prosciutto e melone* is nicely served, with melon that has a perfect degree of ripeness, and prosciutto that is a lovely luscious shade of pink delicately edged in white, but not too fatty or too salty. *Spaghetti pomodoro* and *spaghetti con ragù* are done in the traditional fashion - a light tomato sauce, one without meat and the other with meat - and perfectly cooked pasta. *Rigatoni Amatriciana* is sensational. There is just the right amount of bacon and tomato in the sauce, the smokiness from the bacon providing a winning bass note to the spicy overtones of the dish. *Gnocchi* come with very good *ragù*, but the *gnocchi* themselves are out of this world. They easily pass the test - of being so weightless that with your eyes closed you could not tell if there were any on your fork. They taste wonderful too.

The medallions of pork make a satisfying entrée; they may be prepared with a red wine or an artichoke sauce. *Rombo San Tomà* is turbot prepared with potatoes, tomatoes, olives and capers in a delicate white wine sauce. It is superb with the varied ingredients melding into a harmonious whole. Grilled vegetables make a good *contorno*. Salads are generous, and some entree salads are also available.

For dessert, a piece of almond cake is sweet and macaroony and créme caramel is another fine dessert. The house tiramisù is a better than average rendition of this almost too popular dish. For those who prefer to drink dessert, the *Sgroppino* is on the sweet side yet very refreshing.

There is a surprisingly interesting wine list with nice, inexpensive choices. The Pinot Grigio from Friuli is one of the better wines and is very reasonable. The house red is a little rough but it stands up nicely to a spicy pasta or meat dish; it is better than the house white.

Some of the dishes, such as the *Rombo San Tomà*, are delicious but on the pricey side; you can keep your *conto* down by sticking to the more typical trattoria offerings of which there are many. The current owner and his wife took over from the previous owner about 2 years ago, and they have gradually freshened the decor, and revised the menu and made the place their own. They can be justifiably proud of what they have accomplished.

Antiche Carampane
Rio Terà delle Carampane 1911 | Tel: 041-524-0165

Expensive | *Credit Cards* - *yes* | *Vaporetto* - *San Silvestro*

Open: T - Sat, lunch and dinner; Sun, lunch only
Reservations: recommended for lunch, essential for dinner.

To get there: From the San Silvestro vaporetto stop, walk straight back into Campo San Aponal. Keep walking straight through the campo and cross the Ponte Storto. After the bridge, immediately turn right, and at the next calle another right. When it ends, turn left and the restaurant will be in front of you.

In an area known for its colorful past, this small restaurant can be hard to find, and its clutter of signs stating "No pizza, No lasagna, No telephone, No Tourist Menu," may seem less than friendly. But for those interested in eating well, Antiche Carampane is warm and welcoming. The food is excellent, and you won't find fresher fish anywhere in Venice. In warm weather, you can sit outside under a green and white striped awning across from the amber, yellow and rose hued bricks that make up one of the many beautiful walls in Venice.

Piera will greet and seat you, then Antonia recites the day's offerings; interrupt her too soon and you may miss a treat, but hesitate too long and she will jump in to guide you to a decision. For the intrepid, the mixed seafood antipasto will bring delights from the sea. The chef works magic with *capesante* – scallops. They are usually served gratinée, but are sometimes grilled and are so juicy and luscious that it is impossible not to go back over the shells to scrape every morsel. Another great beginning is a huge bowl of tiny speckled brown *vongole veraci*, sweet and succulent and enlivened with a spicy broth. Soups are also a good choice with the seafood soup being a meal in itself, and the leek soup being a bowlful of flavorful earthy warmth. The delectable assortment of pastas usually includes penne with tuna fish, spaghetti with crab, spaghetti with mixed seafood and spaghetti made black with the ink of the cuttlefish. The staff is more than willing to divide the pasta dishes for two or three people.

For a *secondo*, *branzino* is perfectly grilled with just oil and lemon. The

San Pietro may be lightly breaded and sautéed with artichokes, radicchio, olives, or other delectables. More complex dishes such as *branzino* in a potato crust or *rombo* or *triglie* with *salsa d'agrumi*, a brilliantly colored citrus sauce, are all palate pleasers. The *rombo* for two or more people is a magnificent fish – white and firm and sweetly fresh with a crackling brown skin. In spring and summer, soft shell crabs with creamy polenta are a marvelous combination; the crabs are crunchy and sweet and the polenta is golden and sensuous. Standard sides include french fries, Lyonnaise and boiled potatoes, seasonal green vegetables, grilled radicchio, and green or mixed salad.

Desserts usually include chocolate torte, a fruit tart or pudding, fresh berries in spring and summer and *sgroppino* – one of the best in Venice. A glass of sweet wine with a plate of assorted biscotti is another excellent dessert choice, especially if the plate contains Piera's chocolate "salame."

~~~~~~

When our oldest son, James and his inamorata, Gerarda, joined us in Venice for a visit, we introduced them to Antiche Carampane and our favorite dessert – *sgroppino*, which they greatly enjoyed. We had arranged for them to stay on a few days after we had to leave for home, and one night in their wanderings, they found they were passing Carampane. They had already eaten, but they mentioned having dined there a few nights earlier and asked if they could sit at one of the tables outside and have a *sgroppino*. The *sgroppini* arrived and were every bit as delicious as they remembered.

When they asked for the bill there was a long delay, and then two more *sgroppini* arrived at the table. Although they were a little concerned about the cost, they settled back to enjoy another round of the delicious drinks. Again they tried to get a bill, and this time, after being pointedly ignored for a long time, they saw the restaurant was preparing to close. A final attempt to pay brought only big smiles, the information that there was no bill, and that the *sgroppini* were a gift. When we returned and thanked the staff for their generosity, the smiles we got were as big as the ones on James' and Gerarda's faces when they told us the story. - R.E.

~~~~~~

Osteria Enoteca Vivaldi
Calle della Maddonneta 1457 | Tel: 041-523-8185

Moderate | **Credit Cards -** no | **Vaporetto -** *San Silvestro, San Tomà*

Open: *M - Sat, lunch and dinner*
Reservations: *accepted*

To get there: From Campo San Polo, walk towards Rialto. The restaurant will be on your right.

There is something very inviting about this small and cheerful osteria. The staff is welcoming and very friendly. In winter someone helps diners out of their coats, a courtesy that is rarely extended elsewhere. For an inexpensive, quick bite, you can sit on one of the stools at the bar and look out the window at all the people passing by while you sip a glass of wine and munch on a plate of *cichetti*. If you choose to sit and have a longer meal, you will not be disappointed.

The *pappardelle Vivaldi* is an excellent choice for opening a multi-course meal or as an entree for a simple one. *Spaghetti alla vongole* is also good. For your *secondo*, the *fritto misto* is a delectably crunchy pile of fried sea critters. Tuna with balsamic vinegar is a generous dish with a full-flavored sauce not for the timid. Salads are made with the freshest, crispest ingredients imaginable. Even the rolls at Vivaldi are exceptionally good. Desserts are traditional.

Even though it is clear that all the patrons do not know one another, there is still a neighborhood pub feeling to Vivaldi.

da Sandro

Campiello Meloni 1473 | Tel: 041-523-4894 | Fax: 041-241-1505

Moderate | *Credit Cards* - *yes* | *Vaporetto* - *San Silvestro*

Open: Sat - Th, lunch and dinner
Reservations: recommended

To get there: from Campo San Polo, walk towards Rialto up Calle

Madonnetta. The restaurant is on both sides of the Campiello Meloni.

Da Sandro has been around for 40 years in a small campiello between Campo San Polo and the Rialto. Thinking it looks like a typical tourist trap, you may want to pass it and keep going. Big mistake! This restaurant is off-beat in its physical arrangement and also in its food. The restaurant stands on both sides of the calle; as you face the Rialto, the left side has outdoor benches and tables that are kept warm by a plastic tent in winter and a large dark dining room and bar. The right side has seating for about 16 people in a tiny cozy pizzeria in which you can watch the chef create pizzas as you eat.

You can order pizza or a full dinner in either location. The pizzas are excellent; a spicy sausage with onion and garlic brims with flavor; a prosciutto and arugula polished off with relish by one of the pickiest pizza lovers around, and all the other standards are right on the money.

The regular menu lists several good pasta dishes and the ragù is outstanding. Risotto is excellent with each grain tender and separate yet adding up to that wonderful creamy overall texture of a perfect risotto. A veal cutlet Milanese is crisp on the outside and tender and juicy inside. You will find most of the traditional Venetian specialties on the menu, but the surprise and super attraction of Da Sandro is the beef. Several steak dishes are listed on the menu and every one is worth trying. Any beef lover owes it to him or herself to stop in at Da Sandro for one of their reasonably priced, tender, flavorful and juicy filets cooked precisely as you request it and topped with arugula, parmesan cheese, and balsamic vinegar. The *patate fritte* won't disappoint you either. Salads, though standard in composition, are filled with the freshest ingredients. Breads are fine but if you can wheedle some focaccia out of the pizza chef you are in for a real treat.

The waiters are good humored and cheerful and seem to enjoy running back and forth across the campiello. Prices are beyond reasonable; they are "what a bargain!"

da Ignazio

Calle Saoneri 2749 | Tel: 041-523-4852 | Fax: 041-244-8546

Moderate | *Credit Cards - yes* | *Vaporetto - San Tomà*

Open: Sun - F, lunch and dinner
Reservations: recommended

To get there: From Campo San Polo, walk towards Accademia with the church on your right. From San Tomà, walk towards Rialto. The restaurant is on the main thoroughfare.

The front room of this popular trattoria's windows face the bustling Calle Saoneri; as you eat you can watch tourists wander by with maps clutched in one hand and cameras in the other or locals hurrying home carrying bread, flowers and briefcases. Outside behind sliding glass doors, there is a large leaf covered arbor-like garden.

Among the first courses are a wonderfully hearty vegetable soup, scallops au gratin, excellent *prosciutto e melone*, tiny shrimp served warm with oil and lemon, and a mixed antipasto. Spaghetti with crab, a meltingly rich lasagna, a house special – *spaghetti Trapani* – made with tiny bits of zucchini and eggplant in a tongue-tingling sauce, and spaghetti with *frutta di mare* are among the daily pasta offerings. The grilled fish platter for two has wonderful slightly charred prawns, an excellent piece of *branzino*, *orata* and at least one other fish. For meat lovers, there is veal scallopine, *osso buco* and *fegato alla Veneziana*. The standard *contorni* are available. The *tiramisù* provides a nice contrast of textures and flavors. The *sgroppino* is on the tart side with a generous splash of vodka in it. Crème caramel is consistently good, and sometimes there is a chocolate cake which is as rich and creamy as a mousse. *Macedonie* of fresh fruit is usually available as is a selection of ice cream.

~~~~~~

It was a dark and stormy night – The first night in Venice in a rented apartment instead of a hotel. We had only had a light lunch on the train, and the rain had discouraged us from going food shopping to stock our larder so it was early when we wandered up the calle looking for a place for dinner. Shortly after entering the Calle dei Saoneri, we passed Da Ignazio, a promising looking trattoria. It seemed to be open, but when we entered a waiter asked us to come back in "trenta minuti." We made a reservation for 7:30, and returned to our wanderings up and down the wet calle trying to avoid the serious dripping coming from the eaves above us.

When we returned, we were ushered in and seated just inside the door. We perused the menu, made our choices and sat damply waiting the arrival of the *minestra di verdura* (vegetable soup) which we hoped would be warming. A waiter came over with bread and tried to light the candle. Three times he tried and three times it guttered and went out. On the fourth try, I made a little cupping motion with my hand, and the flame flickered, caught and held, burning brightly. "Ah! La forza della donna!" said the waiter, bowing in my direction.

The next afternoon we walked past Da Ignazio, and our waiter was standing on the front step, smoking a cigarette. As we passed him, his eyes lit with recognition. He made the same little gesture with his hand that I had made to encourage the flame the night before, and then pointed at me and smiled. I felt as though I had made a friend in Venice. - R.E.

~~~~~~

Poste Vecie
Rialto Pescheria Venezia 1608 | Tel: 041-721-822

Expensive | *Credit Cards* - *yes* | *Vaporetto* - *Rialto*

Open: *W - M, 12 - 2:30 p.m. and 7:30 - 10 p.m.*
Reservations: *recommended*

To get there: From the Rialto Bridge, walk straight along Ruga d. Orefici, continue on Ruga d. Speziali. You will come to Campo Beccarie, walk toward the fish market, Poste Vecie will be right in front of you.

Antica Trattoria Poste Vecie, the oldest restaurant in Venice, is housed in a centuries-old post office. Cross over the little humped bridge, and you will be at the front door of Poste Vecie. There is a bar in the entry room with two rooms to the left, and a large enclosed garden room on the right. The two smaller rooms have fireplaces, a rarity in Venice, and they are put to good use on damp winter nights. The walls of the main room are decorated with bills and letters reflecting the fascinating history of Poste Vecie. Poste Vecie has an entrance in the rear for people with disabilities who cannot manage the bridge. As of last year, Poste Vecie has begun renting rooms on the upper floors of the building.

A complimentary Prosecco is delivered by one of the affable and efficient staff; the house wines are better than average and there is an extensive wine list. To start, the *spaghetti con vongole veraci* is outstanding as is a sauté of clams and mussels. *Spaghetti neri* and *spaghetti con frutta del mare* are other popular pastas. The *pasta e fagioli* is one of the best in Venice. Among the *secondi*, one of the *carne* highlights is the *fegato alla Veneziana*, the tender strips of calves' liver often still rosy inside tossed with gently cooked onions and kissed with white wine vinegar. There are several veal dishes, and if there is not one to your liking, the chef will prepare it *come ti vuole* – as you wish. For fish lovers, the *coda di rospo alla griglia* is a sweet and tender version of its cousin, monkfish, and the house *rombo* for two comes with an elegant wine sauce and delicious potatoes which are crisp outside and soft inside. Other dishes are accompanied by small boiled potatoes drizzled with butter, and french fries are always available. Salads and grilled vegetables are other options for your *contorni*. The talented and creative chefs offer an antipasto, *primo piatto* and *secondo piatto* "*del Chef,*" which are spectacularly good dishes. They change very few weeks and are definitely worth exploring.

There is a dessert trolley, which has among other offerings a creamy *tiramisù*. The *sgroppino* is a lovely dessert after a hearty meal. The kitchen also turns out an excellent *panna cotta* with *frutta di bosco*. A delicious *macedonie* of fruit is a light option. A complimentary plate of cookies often shows up with the bill to round off a very pleasant evening and a delicious meal.

Poste Vecie is very old and very "Venetian."

La Perla d'Oriente
Campo dei Frari 3004 | Tel: 041-523-7229

Inexpensive | ***Credit Cards*** - *yes* | ***Vaporetto*** - *San Tomà*

Open: *Daily, continuous service*
Reservations: *accepted*

To get there: The restaurant is in Campo dei Frari.

Though most visitors to Italy are quite content to live solely on Italian food for the length of their stay, it can be fun to explore the way other cuisines are presented in Italy. In Chinese restaurants, there is a charge for every item including tea and rice, and portions are individual rather than family-style. Many Chinese restaurants serve all afternoon and evening so they are good bets if you want to eat early or late.

For a traditional beginning, wonton soup is an unusually rich and flavorful broth with tiny, delicate dumplings, spicy cabbage, and spinach. *Ravioli alla griglia* (grilled dumplings) are tender, juicy and delicious. *Ravioli alla vapore* (steamed dumplings) take a bit longer but are even more exquisitely succulent. *Gamberoni alla griglia* are large prawns grilled so they taste ever so slightly charred; they arrive on a sizzling platter in their shells accompanied by tangy vegetables. Pork with *zai-zai*, a tasty green leafy vegetable, is also good. *Anitra alle erbe* is a sort of hacked duck generously seasoned with herbs – also available is smoked duck. Chicken with mushrooms and bean sprouts is a gentle savory dish for those who do not care for spicy hot food. *Manzo piccante e croccante*, batter dipped shreds of beef, are slightly spicy and crunchy yet they melt in your mouth. There are several dishes *alla piastra*, which arrive at your table on sizzling hot metal platters that have been on or under a flame. The *riso alla Cantonese* is a lightly fried white rice with interesting bits and pieces of meat and vegetables added to it, and the *spaghetti con verdure* is a very thin and delicate noodle stir-fried with vegetables. All the pasta dishes are cooked perfectly *al dente*. The service is uniformly professional and friendly. La Perla D'Oriente also has a pizza menu.

Al Paradiso Ristorante
Calle d. Paradiso 767 | Tel: 041-523-4910

Expensive | *Credit Cards - yes* | *Vaporetto - San Silvestro*

Open: T - Sun, lunch and dinner
Reservations: essential

To get there: From the San Silvestro vaporetto stop, walk straight and then right through the campo until you reach Calle d. Paradiso.

It would be a crime to miss this gem of a trattoria. Giordano's energy and unflagging attention to detail assures diners a rejuvenating experience. The square dining room seats just 24, although the capacity doubles when the weather permits outside dining.

Most standard trattoria dishes are available, with inspired additions. In particular, try an antipasto of *carpaccio* of *branzino* with orange essence, or scallops with baby tomatoes, white wine and thyme. Meat eaters might savor the *Bresaol*a (air dried beef) with an *agrodolce* (sweet and sour) sauce accompanied by a julienne of asparagus.

A *primi piatti* of risotto with shrimp, champagne and grapefruit is over-flowing with fresh sweet shrimp. The champagne and grapefruit add the perfect accents to a dish crowned with a jumbo prawn. *Gnocchetti* with scallops, spider crab and saffron or, for carnivores, with sausage, smoked ricotta and fresh tomato sauce, could easily be an entree. Among the pastas, *spaghetti con vongole veraci* is an excellent version of a classic dish, while *tagliolini* with mushrooms and truffles is perfect for vegetarians or meat eaters.

A bounty of fish can be found on the menu. Crispy *branzino* atop a bed of fennel and endive poached in Pernod is a sublime variation of a familiar Venetian fish. *Pesce San Pietro* prepared with asparagus and gratineed is rich, sensual and utterly satisfying. Tuna with caponata and a salsa verde is tangy and tasty.

Heartier appetites will embrace tender and juicy lamb chops cooked with aged *balsamico,* or for the diet conscious there's a filet of beef with artichokes. Dishes are accented by vegetables of the season and *contorni,* from potatoes to steamed or grilled vegetables to salads.

Don't skip the desserts here. The *panna cotta* is heavenly, and the cold *zabaglione* with crushed *amaretti* under it and fresh berries over it should not be missed. If offered the slightly frizzante moscato with a plate of biscuits, say "yes." The wonderful flavor of the perfectly chilled moscato will convince you that you are indeed dining *al Paradiso*.

~~~~~~

It was a chilly winter's night. Most of the diners at al Paradiso had slightly reddened cheeks - the red that comes from being wind burned, not sunburned. Diners seemed to huddle over the flames of the candles on their tables as if seeking a little extra warmth even though the restaurant itself was toasty. Everyone was dipping into platefuls of warm food and sipping glasses of wine and talking in low murmurs. On the side of the room one young couple was holding hands as they ate; I could catch just enough of their conversation to realize they were not speaking English - Spanish is what I thought I was hearing, but I was not sure.

When their dessert was brought to the table, I followed the plates with my eyes because I love to look at the dishes that are carried past me in restaurants. I enjoy seeing what other people have chosen and I also enjoy seeing the plating. As the *dolce* plates were set down, I could not help but notice the very beautiful young woman was crying. Her long dark hair curtained her face, but I could see both tears and smiles. The young man was leaning towards her, holding both her hands now. I was very curious, but someone else was even more curious than I. Someone called out "did you two just get engaged?"

The young woman blushed; her companion beamed and nodded. "Did he give you a ring just now?" Someone was clearly paying even more attention to this couple than I had been. "Ooh, let's see," another voice said. The young woman, still blushing, crying and smiling, held up her left hand. There was definitely something sparkling on the appropriate finger. The whole restaurant burst into applause.

We learned they were from South America, were visiting Venice for the first time, and the young man had indeed surprised the young woman with a proposal and ring. Many diners asked to buy them drinks, and a wonderful *vino dolce* was poured, but I suspect that no one was charged for the drinks. It was just another evening of magic "al Paradiso." R.E.

Antica Birraria La Corte

Campo San Polo 2168 | Tel: 041-275-0570 | Fax: 041-275-6605

Moderate | **Credit Cards** - *yes* | **Vaporetto** - San Silvestro or San Tomà

Open: daily, lunch and dinner
Reservations: *recommended*

To get there: The restaurant is in Campo San Polo.

A brewery used to be in the building that now houses the restaurant, and the shape of the building was predetermined by the needs of the beer makers. There are huge copper pipes along the ceiling, and lots of wood. There are two kitchens: one is for pizza only and the other handles the rest of the menu. Occasionally this results in some less than perfect timing.

A good way to start a meal is with an appetizer of Pecorino cheese with honey and arugula; the dish is unusual, light and refreshing as well as delicious. A plate of prosciutto is a very simple, very plain and very good way to start.

Among the *primi* courses, *gnocchi al ragù* is a good starter. The gnocchi are little feather pillows which are almost weightless, and the sauce, made with beef and Pecorino cheese, is wonderful. *Bigoli* with an *Amatriciana* sauce that contains Pecorino cheese and a touch of balsamic vinegar gives new flair to a traditional dish. *Tonino alla griglia* is a piece of grilled *tonino* cheese accompanied by two skewers of grilled vegetables. Soup containing celery, leeks, shrimp and chickpeas is wonderful and much more refined than one might expect from its ingredients, which sound hearty. Lightly toasted or roasted chickpeas are scattered across the top and taste like a delicate crunchy nuts.

Pizzas are excellent at Antica Birreria. The Barbarigo is made with a huge pile of thinly sliced roast pork and a lesser amount of eggplant, and the Pasqualingo with artichokes, pork, mozzarella and pecorino is downright spectacular. There is a large assortment of pizzas and special requests are honored.

A secondo of Fettine di Loma, veal slices in a port wine sauce, is extremely tender for its relatively low cost, and the sauce is superb. A pork ribs and sausage plate makes a hearty winter's night treat. Grilled lamb chops come with a side of grilled polenta. The portion is generous - four plump chops - and although the meat is a bit on the tough side they too are bursting with flavor. The *Costata di Angus Irhlandese* is a big thick American style rib steak. It is a bit fatty, but good sharp knives trim the undesired bits away. This steak is sold by weight so the menu price is per unit of weight. Most steaks are three or four times the listed per unit price. It is an easy detail to overlook or forget.

Not unexpectedly, there is a better selection of beer than wine here. Try a lemony Maisel's Weise or a malty Forst Kronen.

There are some interesting items on the dessert menu which leans heavily to dairy based *dolce*. The service can be a little hit or miss; it may take more than one request to get water and the two separate kitchens mean the arrival of dishes is not always perfectly coordinated, but the staff is very pleasant and cheerful, and the food is worth a few minor inconveniences. There is outside seating in the spring and summer.

Circolo alla Buona Forchetta
Calle Perdon 1295 | Tel: 339-650-2086

Moderate | *Credit Cards - no* | *Vaporetto* - San Silvestro

Open: Daily for dinner, occasionally for lunch (call first)
Reservations: strongly recommended

To get there: From Campo San Aponal, walk down Calle Perdon. The restaurant will be on your right.

Amelia Bonvini, owner of the fabulous Bed & Breakfast Corte 1321, turned us on to this one-woman show around the corner from the B & B. Marinella, the chef-owner, cooks everything herself in an exposed, crowded, microscopic kitchen. Marinella is an excellent chef, and everything she puts out is professionally and cleverly plated and served.

On a typical night, you might be served an *amuse bouche* of polenta with "shrimp Livorno" - one plump pink shrimp topped by a slightly spicy red sauce, or a small plate of polenta with spicy seafood. A mixed vegetable appetizer is very appealing with spinach, carrots, an artichoke bottom, a bit of potato and a few other goodies. *Pasta e fagioli* comes in a shallow soup plate with long flat homemade noodles, a thin broth, and lots of beans. *Spaghetti alla Busara* is loaded with fresh sweet shrimp; the sauce is lovely with just a hint of heat in it, and tagliatelle with fish sauce is an outstanding *primo* as is the cannelloni with a meat filling.

Sometimes the menu is a bit quirky. Gnocchi arrive in the pan in which they are prepared - a clever way to keep something as delicate as gnocchi warm - and are delicious although they might be served in a red fish sauce and not cheese sauce as described on the menu. A listed mixed grill fish special is not *"alla griglia"* but is actually far more interesting. Several shrimp are combined with two generous pieces of pan-cooked *Pesce San Pietro* and then napped with a white wine sauce. A spectacular fish soup includes shrimp, tiny squid, clams, mussels, scallops, potato chunks, and a mild white fish (with lots of sharp little bones - the one drawback) all in a clear tomato flavored mildly spiced broth.

Fegato alla Veneziana comes with real polenta, thick, creamy gold and still bubbling from the cook pot. The liver has just the right amount of sautéed onions. Veal scallops are rolled around a tasty stuffing, and covered with tomato sauce and cheese. Grilled prawns are deliciously fresh and sweet although lacking the true charred flavor of the grill. The portion is huge and the meat is loosened so they are very easy to eat.

Salads can be unusual too such one made from *radicchio de Treviso*, beans, potatoes, raw onion and tomatoes tossed with oil and vinegar.

The house wine is not a fine wine but it is very easy to drink; the bottle is unlabelled and you are charged for what you consume. This system makes it easy for people to enjoy both red and white wine with their different courses without having to pay for a whole bottle. There are not many other bottlings available.

Housemade *dolce* are delicious if you have the room. Try a slab of dark and intense blueberry cake topped with chocolate shavings and whipped cream if it is available. A pleasant slightly frizzante dessert wine is usually available too and is served with cookies.

Circolo does not take credit cards so be sure to come with cash. This place is quirky in that what you order is not always exactly what you get, or what you may have expected to get, but we have never had a bad meal there, and Marinella is unfailingly cheerful and helpful. It is off the beaten path both figuratively and literally but well worth a visit.

Ostaria al Garanghelo
Calle dei Botteri 1570 | Tel: 041-721-721

Moderate | *Credit Cards* - yes | *Vaporetto* - San Silvestro

Open: Th – T, lunch and dinner
Reservations: recommended

To get there: From the Rialto bridge, walk straight up Ruga d. Orefici, continue along Ruga d. Speziali and Calle Beccarie, and make a left on Calle dei Botteri. The restaurant will be on your left.

Though they are getting rare, old-school Venetian osterie still exist, and al Garanghelo is proof of that. Located near the fish market, this is one of those places you'll still see the old-timers from the neighborhood coming around for their hourly *ombra*. The long bar in the front can accommodate quite a few of them. There are only a handful of tables and you will be waited on by one of the pleasant, friendly owners. Prices on the menu are all over the place. Most everything is extremely reasonable, but there are a couple of dishes that could move you from "moderate" into "expensive."

Sarde in Saòr are a great starter here, as is a big plate of fresh *soppresata* salami. A mixed vegetable antipasto will meet your daily vegetable needs, with marinated artichoke hearts, grilled tomatoes, sliced potatoes, and some lovely white beans stewed with tomatoes. OK, maybe not your entire vegetable needs, but we like starch.

For your *primi*, pasta with hot pepper and shrimp is an unbeatable starter. It is a simple yet very satisfying dish made – as are all pasta dishes here – with the proper style of pasta for the sauce. *Spaghetti con Vongole* comes with plenty of fresh clams and is just sloppy enough to make one incredibly happy. If seafood is not in the cards, the lasagna has a very rich, almost chorizo-like filling, and it is delicious.

The *primi* are so ample that you might not need to move on to a *secondo*, but it is definitely worth finding some room down there for a melt in your mouth *fegato alla Veneziana*, or a big plate of lightly battered and fried calamari. House wine is good and very reasonable, and there are a few decent, if not over-the-top, bottles available as well.

If you decide to dine at Al Garanghelo, ask the owner to see his "pasta closet" or his collection of postcards sent by happy diners from all over the world. He is a true Venetian keeping a tradition alive, and for that we are grateful.

Taverna San Trovaso
Fondamenta Priuli 1016 | Tel: 041-520-3703

Inexpensive - moderate | *Credit Cards* - yes | *Vaporetto* - Accademia

Open: T - Sun, lunch and dinner
Reservations: recommended

To get there: From the Accademia Bridge, walk right on Calle Gambara and make a left at the first canal. You will be walking right by the restaurant – when you get to the first bridge turn around and you will see the door.

A wonderful stop for lunch or dinner near the Accademia museum, Taverna San Trovaso is popular with both locals and tourists. There are three dining rooms, and the best is downstairs, under a low, black painted brick ceiling – very homey and comforting. The upstairs lacks atmosphere, but generally there are a couple of large parties to create a festive air. The servers all speak some English and are hardworking and helpful.

Taverna San Trovaso is one restaurant that offers a decent Tourist Menu. The selection is huge and the portions are large. Be careful how much you order here, because you probably will have too much. A big bowl of aromatic vegetable soup is a fine start to a meal. Pasta portions are exceptionally hefty, so it might be better to split a pasta if you want a *secondo*. They offer a wonderful *tortellini* with rich cream sauce, peas, and ham – too rich for one, perfect to split. The lasagna is hearty and filling, and for a lighter choice go for the spaghetti with oil, garlic, and hot pepper – simple and delicious. For your *secondo* you might try a plate of perfectly fried scampi, a basic veal steak with lemon, or a beefsteak. Also offered is a large selection of pizzas that, on busy nights, tend to arrive a bit charred. For dessert, try the house *profiteroles* or *sgroppino*.

The house wine is good but there is a list of very good wines at very reasonable prices should you choose to get a bottle.

Locanda Montin
Fondamenta Eremite 1147 | Tel: 041-522-7151 | Fax: 041-520-0255

Moderate - expensive | *Credit Cards - yes* | *Vaporetto - Ca' Rezzonico*

Open: *Th - M, lunch and dinner; T, lunch only*
Reservations: *recommended*

To get there: From Ca' Rezzonico; walk straight back to Campo San Barnaba; go left through the arches and over the bridge. Turn right; the canal will be on your right and buildings on your left. At the next bridge turn left; you do not cross the bridge, but you do have to go up one or two steps. Again the canal will be on your right and buildings on left;

the restaurant is straight ahead.

This is a restaurant with a dual personality. The room's walls are lined with dozens of paintings and drawings, gifts from grateful artists who have been fed, and occasionally housed, by the owners. Fill the long wooden tables with people, and you get a convivial, noisy trattoria. The garden has a different atmosphere. Lined with flowering plants, covered in leaves and filled with bird song, the ambience is gentle, leisurely and languorous even when white-jacketed waiters are racing back and forth with platters of food and every table is taken.

New menus are printed frequently; be sure to check out the ever-changing designs on their backs. Appetizers include standards such as *prosciutto e melone*, excellent pâtés, cold seafood *antipasti*, occasionally a tuna *carpaccio*. *Primi* range from the standard pasta dishes such as spaghetti with ragù to homemade *tortelloni* and an assortment of soups such as *pasta e fagioli* and *zuppa di verdura*. The *tortelloni* are invariably rich and imaginative dishes; the fillings may include radicchio, pumpkin and ground nuts. They are usually generous enough to serve as an entree. The *secondi* also include standard veal and fish dishes, but always feature at least one plate containing beef and often something unusual on Venetian menus such as turkey or duck seasoned with pomegranate. If the *San Pietro con pomodoro e cippoline* is available, try it; the fish is in succulent chunks, lightly browned on the outside, firm, moist and sweet on the inside, with a sauce of onions combined with tomatoes, and a scattering of fennel leaves.

Desserts are often tempting here too. The Antinori Vin Santo with *esse di Buranelle* is an elegant finish to any dinner, but the pear torte captures the essence of pear, and for those who like to indulge there are plenty of rich and gooey treats covered in whipped cream or soaked in liqueurs.

The house wine is excellent and the wine list extensive and varied. Because the Locanda Montin is also a small inn, the restaurant is often open on holidays when other places close.

~~~~~~

One night, accompanied by our daughter, Sarah and our son, Dan, we marched ourselves over to Locanda Montin for dinner. We usually order the house wine, but this night we decided to splurge on an Amarone – that most regal of red wines – and ordered the best one on the menu. It was brought promptly, and we sipped it as we chatted and watched the other diners work their way through various courses. Every now and then, our waiter would tell us our food would be out in a minute.

Finally, after a very long wait and a lot of Amarone, the owner came over to apologize. Somehow our orders had been lost. We went through the menu again because by that time none of us was exactly sure what we had chosen. Then the owner emptied what was left of the wine into our glasses and he said he would bring us another bottle, a gift for our being so gracious about the delay. We protested that it was not really necessary but a fresh bottle of Amarone was being uncorked even as we were speaking.

We were left to enjoy our meal, our second bottle of a magical wine and to wonder what happy fate had caused our order to be misplaced on the same evening we had ordered the best wine in the house. - R.E.

Pizzeria Accademia
Rio Terra Foscarini 878C | Tel: 041-522-7281

Inexpensive | *Credit Cards* - *no* | *Vaporetto* - *Accademia*

Open: *W - M, 7 a.m. - 10:30 p.m.*
Reservations: *not accepted*

To get there: The restaurant is just to the right of the Accademia bridge.

The view from this pizzeria is one of the most incredible in Venice, right under the Accademia Bridge, looking towards the Salute church and the Basin of St. Mark, a panorama of palazzi, boats, sky, and water. Not too many Venetians eat outside here – perhaps because Venetians are not as crazy about the view as visitors are. But Venetians do eat inside, and many stop by the bar to have an *ombra* and to say hello to owners Roberto and Adriano, who have operated this pizzeria for over sixteen years. These are great guys, who, even with a Grand Canal-side dining patio, do not overcharge you to enjoy it.

All the pizza is handmade and cooked by the hard working pizza chef who has been there for many years. The *Pizza Verdure* (vegetable) is a good bet, and depending on what is in season, you might be treated to white asparagus, chucks of ripe tomato, or thin slices of sweet purple onion. The house special is a pleasing mix of salami, mushrooms, onions, and German style sausage. For those with lighter appetites there are good though rather pricey *tramezzini*, and a tasty and filling ham sandwich on a thick roll with a sweet, pink dressing. Beverages are priced a bit higher than at most pizzerias, but the reasonable food prices compensate for this.

The staff is constantly busy and service can be very slow; on the other hand, once you have that fantastic table, it can be yours for hours if you want it. Just sit back, watch the traffic on the Grand Canal and the fevered faces of those waiting to be where you are, and enjoy. The canal-side patio is open even on the coldest of days.

Pier-Dickens Inn

Campo Santa Margherita 5410 | Tel: 041-241-1979

Inexpensive | *Credit Cards* - *no* | *Vaporetto* - *Ca' Rezzonico*

Open: *W - M, lunch and dinner, bar open until 2 a.m.*
Reservations: *not accepted*

To get there: The restaurant is in Campo Santa Margherita

This Italian version of an English pub sits near the entrance of Campo Santa Margherita almost directly across from the famous *gelateria*, Causin. It stands out among other pizza places in the campo as it is mostly patronized by locals and students and has an extensive collection of very good pizzas. In addition to the dining room, there are tables in the campo for use in mild weather, and a huge wooden bar in the front room. The menu offers three pages of pizza possibilities including original creations such as gorgonzola and walnuts. The pizzas are so generously sized, that if accompanied by a salad, one could easily be shared by two people. Try the *Boomerang* topped with onions and garlic; to rev it up even more you can spike it with a dribbling of chili pepper oil. The *Porcellone* is topped with a pile of finely sliced roasted pork and mushrooms. A sprinkling of traditional meat, fish and pasta dishes is also available and there is a good selection of sandwiches. Orders of *patate fritte* are generous and crisply golden brown.

There are four or five beers on tap and lots more available in the bottle. Wine is also available by carafe or by the bottle. An assortment of coffees is listed on the back of the menu.

In the dining area, it is possible to linger over drinks and enjoy the closed-captioned TV, or the music or cabaret-style entertainment that is offered some nights.

Trattoria da Silvio
S. Pantalon 3748-3818 | Tel: 041-520-5833 | Fax: 041-524-4275

Moderate | *Credit Cards - yes* | *Vaporetto - San Tomà*

Open: M - F, lunch and dinner; Sat, dinner only
Reservations: recommended

To get there: From Campo San Tomà, walk down Calle Gozzi, make a right on Crosera, and a left on San Pantalon.

Da Silvio has a delightful garden, which you can enter directly via a gate in a brick wall or by walking through the restaurant. Tables are arranged so you may choose between sunshine and shade, there are trees, flowering plants, and birds singing; and the occasional friendly cat may pass by your table. In sunny but cool weather, there is a pavilion with zip-on sides in which you can sit. There is a pleasant babble of Italian, French, German and English.

A good beginning to a meal is the antipasto of cold meats, an assortment of hams and salamis so generous it can serve as an entree. Prosciutto is available by itself or with melon when it is in season. Mixed grilled vegetables usually consisting of slices of eggplant, zucchini and peppers can be ordered as an antipasto or as a *contorno*. Good *primi* include *tagliatelle* with shrimp and arugula or *tagliatelle* with salmon, and *spaghetti Amatriciana,* a rustic version of this classic with the pancetta and onion cut into a very rough dice. A basic penne with ragù is excellent, and spaghetti with mussels is hearty enough to be a *primo* or an entree. Among the *secondi*, there are grilled scampi with a wonderful smoky, slightly charred taste that comes from cooking over a wood fire and a simply cooked and perfectly boned *branzino alla griglia*. The *bracciole di vitello* is a good choice for meat eaters; it is flavorful and more tender than you might expect it to be. Excellent pizzas with a huge variety of toppings are available at both lunch and dinner.

A *tiramisù* made with chocolate biscotti is among the featured desserts. If you choose a sweet wine, you can pretty much count on a refill. The tab is most reasonable, and the meal, while not haute cuisine, hits the mark.

Trattoria Due Torri

Campo Santa Margherita 3408 | Tel: 041 523-8126

Moderate | **Credit Cards** - *yes* | **Vaporetto** - Ca' Rezzonico

Open: M - Sat, lunch, F & Sat dinner from late spring until autumn
Reservations: *not accepted*

To get there: the restaurant is in Campo Santa Margherita.

If you want to eat like and with the locals, this is a good place to do it. The restaurant is bigger than it looks - there are tables outside, and inside, a bar and more tables and also a back room with space for many more people. Decor is minimal and the ambience is relaxed and friendly with many people from the community sitting quite happily alongside hungry tourists.

The menu is written on a large portable board, which is carried from table to table. The waiters speak excellent English and are happy to explain or describe the dishes in Italian or English. Penne with *radicchio* and *pancetta* makes a delicious and rich beginning. For a more traditional start, try the gnocchi with ragù; although the gnocchi are unusually large, they are light and not gummy. With a meaty and slightly spicy sauce the gnocchi make a hearty, but not overwhelming *primo* and a satisfying entree.

Among the *secondi*, grilled fish are done simply and traditionally here. Both the whole *branzino* and *orata* look wonderful on the platter, but they will be boned for you unless you prefer to do it yourself. An old Venetian fisherman's technique is used after the boning is completed. First, lemons are squeezed over the heads, tails and bones; then olive oil, salt, pepper, the lemons themselves, and a little white wine vinegar are added to the platter. Using two spoons, the waiter deftly masses everything together, until finally, he tilts the platter so the juices and oil run down to a corner where they mingle with bits of chopped herbs that had been on the fish.

This juice is spooned over the filleted fish. Heavenly!

Meat lovers can satisfy their cravings with a grilled steak, which will come cooked *al sangue* if that is requested. A generous order of crisp fries comes with the steak.

The usual trattoria desserts are available as well as a good assortment of *vino dolce* including a *fragolino* and a *passito* from Sicily. The dessert wines come with a little plate of cookies.

At lunch, Due Torri is a working man's spot, but everyone is relaxed and friendly, and the food - especially the fish - is reasonably priced and super-fresh. Children are not only welcome; they are indulged.

Ca' Foscari Al Canton
Crosera 3854 | Tel: 041-522-9216

Moderate | Credit Cards - *no* **| Vaporetto -** *San Tomà*

Open: *Daily, lunch and dinner*
Reservations: *accepted*

To get there: From the San Tomà vaporetto stop: bear left at the end of the calle and cross the bridge. Turn right and walk along the canal. It will look as though you are approaching a solid wall, but you can turn left just before you run into the wall. At the end of this calle, turn right and the restaurant is just ahead on the left.

This small and unpretentious user-friendly trattoria offers simple but excellent food. There is a bright and cheerful room to your right as you enter, and to the left, just past the dessert case, there is a larger room decorated with paintings of Venice including a pair "painted" with crushed glass.

Pastas are a good way to open a meal. The Romagnoli classic, *spaghetti Bolognese* is well done here as is *spaghetti con vongole veraci* or spaghetti with squid ink. Even a basic spaghetti with *salsa di pomodoro* hits the mark. The *lasagna al forno* deserves and draws raves and the *risotto primavera*, made for two, is an excellent non-pasta option. For those who prefer *minestra* for a first course the vegetable soup is a hearty beginning. Among the meat entrees the *braciola di maiale* (pork chop), and the grilled veal chop are well, and simply, prepared. The *costolette di vitello* Milanese is outstanding with a crisp outside and a tender juicy inside. Among the seafood entrees, the *scampi alla griglia* are especially noteworthy, the prawns lightly charred and deliciously smoky. The *patate fritte* are invariably greaseless and crisp although sometimes a little too generously salted. The grilled vegetables are a generous assortment of brightly colored peppers and gently charred eggplant, zucchini and sometimes radicchio.

The wine list is small but varied. Among the *dolce* is an outstanding almond cake, a light and not overly sweet *pasta sfoglia*, a *Torte della Nonna*, which is rich with ricotta cheese, and chocolate *profiteroles*. The servers are friendly and helpful; the atmosphere is casual. Occasionally a complimentary *limoncello* arrives with the check although it is certainly not needed to cushion the blow because this trattoria offers better than average food at very reasonable prices.

Casin dei Nobili
Calle d. Casin 2765 | Tel: 041-241-1841

Moderate | *Credit Cards - yes* | *Vaporetto - Ca' Rezzonico*

Open: T - Sun, lunch and dinner
Reservations: accepted

To get there: From Ca' Rezzonico, walk straight towards Campo San Barnaba, at the Campo make a left on Calle d. Casin. The restaurant will be on your right.

The decor of Casin dei Nobili is a funky, appealing clutter of art and artifacts; and an outdoor eating area is offered in warmer months.

The menu changes seasonally. If available, *capesante* with porcini mushrooms are excellent with lots of delectable porcini bits decorating the juicy scallops. Another seafood appetizer is *schie con polenta*. The *schie* (tiny brown shrimp) are good enough but the polenta is sensational. Draw a forkful of the *schie* into the pool of polenta so they are clothed with gold and indulge in a treat that is so flavorful and so sensuous it is downright seductive. For meat eaters, the smoked goose breast is delicate tasting and comes in a very generous portion. It looks raw, but tastes cooked; it has a slightly smoky flavor that resembles pastrami. An unusual first course is cheese with truffles and truffle honey. *Pasta e fagioli* is properly hearty and filling. The *gnocchi con rucola e speck* is a rich and tasty first course, and the *pappardelle Mantovani* – a ragù with ground meat, peas, carrots and other vegetables, but no tomato – is especially delicious.

Among the *secondi*, look for the special seafood in parchment served for two or more. Two huge plates piled with mussels, clams, *canocche*, *branzino* and *orata* are surrounded by a pleasant mildly piccante sauce. For those wanting a lighter entree the grilled *coda di rospo* – monkfish – is a nice choice. The *cinghiale*, wild boar, is prepared like a stew or braised meat; it is earthy and filling – good fare for a winter's night. Some nights duck appears on the menu and is often accompanied by whole onions, which are mild and lusciously sweet. Another tasty but messy choice is the *agnello al forno*. The lamb is a generous portion of what can best be described as hacked lamb. It is impossible to get much meat without picking the bones up and gnawing away on them, but it is worth the effort. Among the *contorni*, the potato croquettes are especially delicious; they are crisp outside and creamy inside. Entree salads are available and are universally crispy, crunchy and full of goodies. The pizzas, ordered from a separate menu, are eagerly consumed.

Sgroppino is a cool and refreshing dessert after a hearty meal. Crêpes with chocolate are available for those who want to splurge on their *dolce*.

Limoncello or port are alternatives to sweets.

The servers are young, friendly and cheerful and most speak better English than they will admit; they are unduly modest. Even when the place is packed they never lose their cool or their smiles.

Arca Ristorante-Pizzeria
Calle San Pantalon 3757 | Tel: 041-524-2236 Fax: 041-244-8581

Moderate | *Credit Cards - yes* | *Vaporetto - San Tomà*

Open: M – Sat, lunch and dinner
Reservations: recommended

To get there: from the San Tomà Vaporetto, walk back along the calleand turn left. Cross the bridge and turn right. Walk along the Rio and go left. Make the first right and walk along the Crosera to Calle San Pantalon. Arca is on your right as you walk towards Campo San Pantalon.

This easy-going, pleasant restaurant is next to the bar of the same name, which is a great place to stop off for an afternoon coffee or snack. On the other side of the restaurant there is a new gourmet food shop run by the same people. The bar is fairly utilitarian, and the restaurant has simple white washed walls that melt into dark paneling and a low-beamed ceiling. The front rooms have colorful murals depicting scenes from Noah's Ark and there is a small back room that used to be the no-smoking room; it is decorated with two paintings of an elephant and a flamingo and diners there run the risk of being forgotten - at least temporarily.

Arca is not a white tablecloth elegance sort of place. Don't come here for glamour or great bread. The tables are bare wood with paper placemats and napkins, but the menu boasts several interesting dishes.

There are many pizzas offered at Arca and pizza is excellent here. The pizza with grilled radicchio as a topping has a rather bland sauce but the flavor of the radicchio is terrific. The Diavolo is appropriately hot and spicy without being overdone.

There is also a separate section of crepes, which can be eaten as a *primo* or *secondo*. The Laguna Crepe contains seafood, tomato sauce and cheese. The crepe itself is excellent and the filling is tasty and rich with lots of cheese.

If you are in the mood for a few courses, vegetable soup is a simple hearty way to start a meal especially on a cold night. *Spaghetti con vongole veraci* is served in a traditional manner and is very good. In an unusual presentation the tiny clams are arranged in a circle around the pile of pasta, which has a nicely balanced sauce of oil, garlic, and parsley. *Spaghetti Scaligero* has an oil-based sauce loaded with chunks of fresh tomato, pink shrimp, tiny clams in their shells, and plump succu-lent mussels in their gorgeous blue black shells. A little *peperoncini* adds some heat, which really perks the sauce up. A scallop risotto with saffron takes the usual 20 minutes to arrive and is worth the wait. The rice is at the magic point between being too *al dente* and too mushy; the scallops - the coral part included - are fresh and sweet, and the saffron adds a slightly earthy undertone to the whole dish, pulling it together.

The pork filet with port wine and juniper berries is an unusual and consistently good *secondo*. The *Fiorentina* steak is not exactly *Fiorentina* in style - we'd call it a filet - but it is full of hearty beef flavor and is very tender. It is also cooked perfectly *al sangue* as requested, and is accompanied by spicy green and mild red sauces. The grilled meat plate is a very generous offering; it consists of a lamb chop, a beef filet, a veal chop, and a spicy sausage. Skewered grilled lamb consists of twelve skewers of tiny pieces of smoky, tasty lamb.

A grilled fish platter for two typically comes with a good sized piece of *branzino*, nicely boned and perfectly grilled, a tender and delicately flavored piece of monkfish, a filet of salmon and/or sole, a small *orata* and a giant prawn from which the meat has been loosened for easy access. Extremely reasonably priced for its quantity and quality, this dish is a real bargain.

The wine list offers some goodies such as a Nebbiolo d'Alba, which works really well with the spicy sauces used on the pastas and pizzas. The house wine is drinkable, but nothing over the top.

Dessert choices are limited; the *tiramisù* is more interesting than most, and the *profiteroles* are rich and satisfying. The servers may seem a bit less polished than some, but they are friendly and very efficient. The ambience is casual; families with children are really welcome here, and the food is first rate.

Cantinone Storico
Rio San Vio 660/661 | Tel: 041-523-9577 Fax: 041-277-6877

Moderate - expensive | *Credit Cards -* yes | *Vaporetto -* Accademia

Open: M – Sat, lunch and dinner
Reservations: strongly recommended

To get there: The restaurant is just off Campo San Vio.

Cantinone Storico has the sort of casual and comfortable ambience that makes you feel you will be well taken care of. The décor is simple but pleasing to the eye. The walls are washed by light from simple but pretty flower-shaped lumineres, and brightened by a series of paintings by the owner. On balmy nights tables are set outside along the canal.

You are welcomed with a complimentary glass of Prosecco. If you love seafood, a good start to a meal is the sauté of mussels and clams served in a large bowl. Try eating them the Venetian way, not with a fork but with the hands. Break off the top shell and then use the bottom half to scoop up some of the broth from the bottom of the bowl, and then just slurp it all out. Tuna carpaccio, thin slices of a gorgeous pink almost the color of watermelon, is presented over fresh baby arugula and is as appealing to the eye as it is to the palate. Prosciutto and melon pairs top quality prosciutto with perfectly ripe cantaloupe or other melons of the season.

Cicale di mare, also known as *canoce* or *canocchie*, are crayfish and may be enjoyed as an antipasto with just oil and lemon, or as a *primo piatto* in a red sauce on spaghetti. Other good pasta choices are the *spaghetti con vongole veraci* and the *spaghetti con granchio*. *Risotto terra e mare* comes with shrimp and either asparagus or artichokes and is delicious and well worth the wait.

The mixed grilled fish entree for two arrives on huge plates rimmed with pink and decorated with tiny flowers. A typical offering might be pieces of sole, *orata*, *branzino*, and giant scampi. Each fish retains its unique favor and each is excellent. The *rombo con patate* is a lovely piece of turbot and is served with delicious potatoes with a cheese topping.

Carnivores will enjoy the veal dishes, with Marsala and with *limone*. The chicken cacciatore, a dish not seen often in Venice, has a rich and savory sauce that contains incredibly sweet carrots and chunks of tomato. It begs to be mopped up with a generous hunk of bread. *Fegato alla Veneziana* is a sturdy rendition of this classic.

Among the *contorni, patate fritte* come in an enormous mound and are crisp and not too salty. The seasonal vegetables are another good choice. The platter might include lightly grilled rounds of eggplant, potatoes which are crisp outside and so soft inside they are almost pureed, wonderfully smoky grilled *radicchio del Treviso*, zucchini slices that melt in the mouth, a mound of sautéed red and yellow peppers that taste like summer even in April and/or a zesty *caponata*.

House wine is decent, but can be on the frizzante side, and there are some nice choices on the wine list. The bread basket is worth exploring, with some good breadsticks and nice rolls - crunchy outside and soft enough inside to sop up sauces.

If you have room for *dolce*, a slab of chocolate cake is outstandingly moist and tender although the overall flavor is simply sweet as opposed to intensely chocolate. *Sgroppino* is refreshingly cool, smooth and sweet but only mildly lemony. If the meringue is available, go for it; it is sinfully good. If rich desserts are not your style there is an interesting selection of dessert wines on the wine list.

The staff all speak good English and are very friendly, helpful and thought-ful. For what it is worth, a high proportion of the guests seem to be Americans and Brits. Cantinone Storico is a very professional, smoothly run restaurant with reasonable prices and very good food, but there is also something very homey and cozy about it.

Ristorante Riviera

Zattere 1473| Tel: 041-522-7621 Fax: 041-244-7724

Expensive | Credit Cards - *yes* **| Vaporetto -** San Basilio

Open: *T - Sun, lunch and dinner*
Reservations: *essential*

To Get there: from the vaporetto stop at San Basilio, make a right on the Zattere. The restaurant is a short distance ahead.

This jewel box of a restaurant greatly expands its capacity in balmy weather when it is possible to dine outside along the Giudecca Canal. There is a bar and a semi-open kitchen in the rear; the main seating area is enhanced by large and beautiful photographs of Venice, and lighted mirrored recesses which house some lovely wine glasses, wine bottles and a few other bits and pieces.

The menu is small, but every item on it is tempting. You are welcomed with a complimentary glass of Prosecco. The bread basket contains several tasty treats all made by Chef Monica, and when it is almost empty, it is whisked away and replaced with a full basket - something that rarely happens in Venice.

The star of the antipasti is the tuna tartare, whether it is served with avocado or zucchini, and it is a sublime start to any meal. *Gamboretti* with polenta is excellent; the tiny shrimp are lovely and fresh, and the polenta is sensational. Asparagus with egg and Parmigiano is a very good, very light beginning as is the *gransèola*, fresh spider crab, which is presented with a dollop of roe on top.

An extraordinary *primo,* when it is available, is the *taglialini* with scallops and artichokes. It is a wonderful pasta perfectly sauced with plenty of succulent pieces of scallop and tender green artichoke leaves. The *bigoli in salsa* with its sauce of anchovies and onions is intense and bursting with flavor, while the *bigoli* with chicken is a gentle and soothing dish. Ravioli filled with potato and accompanied by *triglie*, which is red mullet, is another fabulous *primo.*

Among the *secondi* are a buttery *Pesce San Pietro with carciofi* - tiny whole artichokes, and an unusual and delicious *spiedini* of calamari and monkfish wrapped in bacon with caramelized shallots and radicchio. The calamari are tender and sweetly flavorful; the bacon wrapped *coda di rospo* is smoky and tender. The *radicchio de Treviso* is perfectly grilled; its slightly charred flavor blends perfectly with the bacon while the shallots caramelized in balsamico are tangy and sweet. It is a unique combination very skillfully put together and perfectly executed.

Rombo is a simple but elegant dish when accompanied by tiny whole artichokes and lightly cooked sweet fresh asparagus. A few slices of potato make it a complete meal. It is very satisfying without being overly filling. The platter of mixed grilled fish wins points for presentation as well as flavor.

Fegato alla Veneziana has tender meat and sweet onions, and is a first rate version of this Venetian favorite. The lamb chops with blueberry sauce are a match made in heaven, and must be tasted to be believed. Veal with asparagus is another lovely entree. There are three slices of veal - two are just plain veal napped with an excellent sauce while the third is wrapped around several spears of tiny tender asparagus.

Among the *dolce*, the tiny pears poached in wine sauce are so fabulous they hardly even need the fine homemade vanilla gelato that comes with them. *Panna cotta* is sinfully rich and delicious, and the *tiramisù* is several cuts above the typical presentation.

The wine list is excellent, and offers some unusual selections. Chef Monica must be part sorceress to be able to turn out so many wonderful dishes in her tiny kitchen and her debonair husband, Luca, is a delightful front man and tries to give every diner the best Riviera has to offer. The witty Alessandro delivers your dishes with panache.

~~~~~~

One of the many delectable dishes that Chef Monica prepares at **Ristorante Riviera is Lamb Chops with *Mirtilli* (blueberry) sauce.** Martin and I love lamb, and when we saw it on the menu, even though we could not imagine this particular combination, we did not hesitate to try it. After one bite, we knew we had found a new favorite, and ordered it whenever we saw it on the menu.

It is a justifiably popular dish, and often by the time we placed our order, there was no more lamb left for us. I began inquiring about the dish when I made reservations, and if it was on the menu, I would ask if they could hold two portions for us. Then the season changed, and blueberries were not available so the lamb with blueberries disappeared from the menu, and was replaced with lamb in a Barolo wine sauce, a delicious if slightly less unusual dish.

One night we sat down for dinner, and as we studied the menu, we saw the lamb chops were being offered with the Barolo wine sauce. We ordered our *primi* and then the lamb for our *secondi*. While we were enjoying our first courses, Luca came over with a twinkle in his eye and asked us how we wanted our lamb chops prepared. It took a minute but by the third time he asked, with an impish grin on his face and that twinkle in his eye, the penny dropped, and I said, "*Mirtilli? É possible stasera?*" "*Si*!" Luca replied. We were delighted - and impressed that he remembered how much we had loved the lamb chops with blueberries on our previous visits. He told us that Monica had found some blueberries to serve with *panna cotta*, and remembering how much we liked the lamb with them, and seeing that we had a reservation for that night, she had saved some to make a sauce for our lamb. It was even more fantastic than usual because it was a "special" - just for us.

Osteria La Zucca
Ponte del Megio 1762 | Tel: 041-524-1570

Moderate | *Credit Cards* - yes | *Vaporetto* - San Stae

Open: M - Sat, lunch and dinner
Reservations: essential

To get there: From San Stae, walk straight up Salizzada San Stae and make a right on Calle del Tintor.

One of the most interesting restaurants in Venice, La Zucca serves up delicious food at incredibly reasonable prices. It may be the out of the way location that keeps the prices low, but whatever it is, the food is always fresh, excellent, and often very rich. The dining room has paneled walls and wooden tables, and there are a few outside tables overlooking a graffiti covered wall.

The menu changes every day, but there are a few standbys. For starters, if available, don't miss the rich and flavorful pumpkin soup. It is one of the best dishes in Venice. A pumpkin flan topped with spiked shards of aged ricotta cheese is another good choice. Pasta is a great starter if you want to have a *secondo*, but is also rich and filling enough to satisfy on its own. The lasagna with radicchio, mushrooms and *speck* or lasagna with artichokes are both creamy, plate-licking renditions. Penne is usually available with a variety of sauces, like fresh tomato, ricotta and basil or buttery Gorgonzola. *Pizzocheri* is whole-wheat pasta layered with cabbage, béchamel sauce and sharp cheese, and we dare you to finish the whole thing. Meat menu options usually have a global theme, such as lamb tagine with couscous, or steak with guacamole. Carnivores will also be quite happy with a dish of sliced pork covered in a light and tasty mustard sauce. Vegetables shine at La Zucca, and it is easy to go a little crazy on the *contorni*. Be careful, everything is so rich, you may end up with too much food. The stuffed zucchini could be an entrée in itself and curried carrots are zesty and hot. Gratins of potato and cauliflower are especially delicious and rib sticking. The green salad is one of the best in Venice.

The desserts are fantastic and there is a little argument between the authors about which is the best, the chestnut mousse or the *panna cotta* drizzled with honey and sprinkled with nuts. Both are ambrosial. Other choices might be a strawberry Bavarese, apple cake, or an orange *macedonie* with dried fruits that has an amazingly good combination of flavors and textures. The wine list is full of well priced, hard-to-find wines from small producers, and the house wine is also good.

The servers are uniformly pleasant and helpful, but service can be slow, especially waiting for the check. You can always finish the last dregs of wine or try to lick a bit more chestnut mousse off your spoon. Reservations are a must.

Pizzeria Ae Oche
Calle delle Tintor 1552 | Tel: 041-524-1161

Inexpensive | *Credit Cards - yes* | *Vaporetto - San Stae*

Open: *T - Sun, lunch and dinner*
Reservations: *not accepted*

To get there: From Campo San Giacomo dell' Orio, walk down Calle delle Tintor.

This popular pizzeria is packed day and night with locals and tourists who come to sample from the huge menu of creative pizzas. The dining room looks like an old barn and is covered with American advertising posters from the early 1900s, and the effect is very comforting and cozy. Not comforting, but delicious, is the *Mangiafuoco* (eat fire), covered with four hot sauces and hot sausage, and not for the weak-kneed. There are many other tasty options that won't set your mouth on fire, such as the *Sfiziosa* with pesto, pine nuts and arugula, or you can build your own pizza. A small selection of pasta and meat dishes is also offered.

House wine is OK, but beer and soft drinks are a better choice here, or spring for a bottle of Chianti.

Ae Oche recently opened a second location on the Zattere, at Dorsoduro 1414.

Il Refolo
Campiello del Piovan 1459 | Tel: 041-524-0016

Moderate - expensive | *Credit Cards - yes* | *Vaporetto - San Stae*

Open: T - Sun for dinner, W – Sun lunch (open April through October only.)
Reservations: recommended

To Get there: The restaurant is behind the church of San Giacomo dell' Orio.

Il Refolo is owned by the Martin family, who also own the famous restaurant da Fiore, and it is run by the son, Damiano Martin. It is a warm weather restaurant, and most of the tables are outside along a canal - a peaceful, romantic setting. Damiano Martin seems to be there every night, running around setting up tables, greeting people, and taking orders. The rest of his staff is efficient and friendly and they all speak some English. Start with one of their uber-sized Spritzes while you peruse the menu.

Il Refolo calls itself a pizzeria, but they also have other menu items worth noting. You might try a smooth pumpkin soup flavored with porcini mushrooms and a hint of cream. Lasagna topped with blueberries is very basic, but with a tart twist. Mussels with either red or white sauce are plump, juicy and sassy with flavor. The red sauce is perfection, with just enough heat, spice, fragrance and flavor. The *Insalata Caprese* made from sliced tomatoes and buffalo milk mozzarella is more than enough for two people as is the plate of prosciutto, coppa and salami. *Rigatoni Il Refolo*, which is prepared with vegetables, cream and cheese, is a perfect example of a *primo* which can also serve well as an entree.

If you are getting sick of Italian food, try Il Refolo's chicken curry - half a chicken in a spicy curry sauce, with basmati sauce and an extremely hot *raita* on the side. Among the other *secondi* it is hard to beat the succulent grilled lamb chops which form a tent over some fabulous potatoes. The *tagliata* of Angus Irlandese – Irish beef - is very good and the spinach that accompanies the steak tastes like spinach and not like garlic as it sometimes does.

The pizza at Il Refolo is among the best in Venice. The pizza with figs and *proscuitto* is out of this world, every bite carrying with it a new sensation. If you like figs, this is a must-try. Other options include gorgonzola with speck or a vegetarian pizza covered with various seasonal toppings. Pizza lovers should be aware that not all the specialty pizzas are available all year round; those that use seasonal toppings are made only when the fresh ingredients are can be procured.

The house wine is a little on the pricey side but is very drinkable. The bottle selection is small, but well-chosen, and there are some interesting beers offered.

For dessert, you can't go wrong with *sgroppino* here, but if you want to get even more decadent, try the *panna cotta*, which comes covered with a variety of toppings, such as berries or *Zabaione*. *Torte au cioccolato* is rich and satisfying, but nothing unusual or spectacular; on the other hand, the *zuppa de mele*, which is like a vanilla scented apple sauce served over strawberries, blueberries, blackberries, raspberries and thinly sliced almonds, is a lovely, light and unusual *dolce*.

Il Refolo is a local's pizzeria with four-star service and a creative touch. If you are in Venice during the warmer months, Damiano Martin and his staff won't disappoint you.

~~~~~~

On my first trip to Venice after the first edition of Chow! Venice was published, I entertained thoughts of treating myself to da Fiore, one of Venice's "best" restaurants. I had read before I left, however, about Il Refolo, the pizzeria owned by the same family. On my second night, all thoughts of da Fiore left my mind, and I found myself walking to Il Refolo.

As a single diner (and a woman to boot) I am always looking for that perfect place to dine alone. Often, I am turned away, or put at a table in a corner and somewhat ignored. Not at Il Refolo. When I arrived that first night, the restaurant was full, but Damiano Martin, the owner, immediately came over and led me to a table. I ordered a Spritz to sip on while I perused the menu. While I sipped on my Spritz a waiter came over to ask what I wanted to eat, but I didn't want to order until I finished my Spritz. Finally, Damiano Martin came over and asked me what I wanted, and I told him I really wanted to finish my Spritz first.

"I tell you what," he said. "I will let no one bother you until you finish your Spritz."

I pretty much fell in love right there. To me, this is what great service is all about.

On that night, and two others on that trip, I watched Damiano Martin in action. He was constantly moving – taking orders, talking to people, making sure everyone was happy. On my second visit, the restaurant was full, but he told me – a single diner – to wait a minute, then he and a waiter rolled a tabletop out of the restaurant and set it up for me, right then and there! I thought that was pretty cool, and I will never forget the gesture, or those first delicious meals, that I had at Il Refolo.

~~~~~~

Al Nono Risorto

Campo San Cassiano 2337 | Tel: 041-524-1169

Inexpensive - moderate | **Credit Cards -** *yes* | **Vaporetto -** *San Stae*

Open: Th –T lunch and dinner
Reservations: *not needed*

To get there: the restaurant is just off Campo San Cassiano.

Sitting at a table at Al Nono Risorto, you might be reminded of all the other bohemian places you have eaten in over the years. There is a slight sense of chaos, but everything runs smoothly. The owners and staff (and most of the diners) don't give a flip about fashion. The kitchen is open late, and between the Santa Croce location and the local crowd, you'll definitely feel like relaxing and taking it all in here. There is a large dining room, and in warm weather, you can sit outside in a pretty garden.

There is a Venetian menu and some good starters, such as a big plate of thinly sliced prosciutto, but we go to Al Nono Risorto for the pizza. The pizzas are wonderful here – they come out of the kitchen steaming hot and cooked with not only love, but bohemian love.

Desserts are standard, and good, hearty, yet cheap beverages are offered. *Sgroppino* or grappa are a good way to finish a meal here. This is a great place to eat not only for the late hours, but for the atmosphere, because if there are other tourists there, you probably won't hear them. They host a chess club a couple of nights a week.

A Guide to Venetian Bars

"The bar" is a very important part of Venetian, and Italian, life. The Italian bar is a meeting place, a spot to have morning coffee and read the paper, to munch on a sandwich at lunch, to have an evening glass of wine and talk about the day with friends. Venice has no cars, so people get around mainly by foot. They can't spend hours talking to one person every time they run into someone they know, so a good way to catch up yet make a fairly quick exit is to run into the nearest bar for an espresso or a glass of wine. There are a large number of bars in Venice, most offer something for everyone, but there are some that are better than others. Some are fair, some will cheat you; some have great wine by the glass, some serve swill; some are full of college students, some are gondoliers hangouts. They are a haven for tourists who just can't walk anymore and need a beverage and a restroom. This is your guide to the best bars in many categories.

All Venetian bars offer coffee, water and wine. Most offer morning pastries and lunchtime snacks ranging from a half dozen *tramezzini* to large selections of *tramezzini*, *panini*, pastas, pizzas, and other dishes. Some have *cichetti* and all have Spritz. When ordering at a Venetian bar, you pay much less standing up, and all posted prices can double or even triple if you sit down. The bars we list here have been selected not only for their appeal but also for their sway towards honesty, but if you ever feel you are being overcharged, do not hesitate to question them and always get a receipt. If you are a night owl, we can steer you in the right direction, but keep in mind that bars close when they want to, not according to the posted hours. We have not included phone numbers in the bar section.

Caffè Florian Piazza San Marco	***Open:*** Th - T, 9:30 a.m. - Midnight

To get there: The bar is in Piazza San Marco

How much you enjoy Florian will depend in part on your reason for going there. If you go there for the experience, you will no doubt enjoy it much more than if you are going there for the food or drink. A winter tea, served in a beautifully decorated room with well-padded chairs and small sofas at which elegantly-clad waiters serve you with exquisite care, launches you straight into the Belle Epoch. You get a selection of tiny sandwiches, scones, jam and tiny pastries as well as the tea of your choice placed before you. There are fine china plates and cups, matching tea pots, crisp napery and everything tastes – just okay. A summer espresso or vino in the Piazza San Marco can be equally splendid. Sit at one of the small tables under a sparkling blue sky and a smiling sun and watch the pigeons dive and swoop, children run and play, and the adults, with their cameras in hand, snap away at everything in sight, and you feel you are part of a postcard setting. Come at night when the moon beams down on you from a dark sky with mystical swirls of clouds and a sprinkling of stars, and you can feel time stand still. Didn't Casanova stop here for one last coffee after fleeing the prison adjacent to the Doge's Palace? Music from the orchestra makes you want to linger for just one more sip, and your drink is accompanied by a small bowl of savory treats, a carafe of water, and a neatly printed list of the items you can buy with the Florian imprint. Though pricey, everyone should do this once; but it really is your choice – ambience or economy.

There is one way you can have both. Enter Florian, walk past the huge curving staircase and stop at the bar. Order your coffee or wine and hope that one of the small tables with little chairs around it is available. Carry your beverage – and the little plate of cookies that may come with it - over to the table, sit down and enjoy Florian for much less than in the inner sanctum or outer piazza. It's still a bit more than the average coffee bar but then so is Florian.

| **Cavatappi** | ***Open:*** T - Sun 9 a.m. - 11 p.m. |
| Campo della Guerra 525/526 | Closed Sun night. |

To get there: From Piazza San Marco, walk under the clock tower onto Merc d. Orologio, make a right through Campo San Zulian which puts you into Campo della Guerra. The bar will be on your left.

This bar has a lot going for it. It is near Piazza San Marco; it is open late; it has a great list of wines by the glass; it has good, unique sandwiches and great cheeses and meats to try with your wine. The wine list changes every two months and features a different region of Italy each time. Cheeses from the same region are also offered. A lunch with one or two set menus of the day is served for about 10 Euro. The young owners are bringing a breath of fresh air to the area with all these great ideas, and it seems to be paying off as the place is packed every evening with Venetians trying cheeses from Friuli or cured wild boar from Tuscany. The staff all speak English and don't overcharge. The bar is adjacent to a hotel, and customers may use the modern and spotless hotel restrooms.

Thursday through Saturday, a *crudo* (raw) menu is featured for both fish and meat for 15 Euro. Cavatappi also offers a breakfast menu with eggs and bacon, in case you need a fix.

Lowenbrau Bar
Rialto Bridge, San Marco side

Open: Th - T, early until 11 p.m. or so

To get there: The bar is at the foot of the Rialto bridge on the San Marco side.

You pay a premium to sit outside at this tourist-packed bar, but if you score the right table, it is worth it. You sit with your back against a five-hundred-year-old bridge and one of the world's most stunning views in front of you. In the daytime, the spectacle of delivery guys throwing boxes across four boats and near fights between taxi drivers and gondoliers makes for interesting viewing. On weekend nights, when the Grand Canal becomes El Camino Real, Lowenbrau Bar is a great place to observe it. Kids in their speedboats, rich people in taxis, tourists in gondolas – it is magical. They don't call it the "Grand" Canal for nothing, and Lowenbrau Bar is a great place to hang out and observe Venice's life and energy.

Alla Botte
Calle della Bissa 5482

Open: F- W, 10 a.m. - 3 p.m. and M, T, F and Sat, 6 p.m. - 11p.m.

To get there: Find the public restroom in Campo San Bartolomeo and walk past it and around the corner.

One of the best bars in town for *cichetti* and wines by the glass, Alla Botte is always packed with Venetians and tourists in-the-know. Try a plate of assorted seafood *cichetti* with a glass of Soave, or a slice of ham and potato pie with a glass of Tokai, or meatballs and sliced salami with a Pinot Nero or Barbera. There is a room to sit and have larger meals, but all the action is at the bar. It can get quite crowded and smoky outside in the calle.

Moscacieka
Calle Fabbri 4717

Open: M - Sat, 10 a.m. - Midnight

To get there: From the Rialto Bridge, walk down the Grand Canal to Calle Bembo. Calle Bembo turns into Fabbri, the bar will be on your left.

This unpretentious, youthful bar sits on one of the main arteries between Rialto and Piazza San Marco. Good wines by the glass and a great CD collection are highlights. There is a large room in the back perfect for observing young Venetians in their native habitat, and lots of young couples seem to come here to make out or fight. A little bowl of salty stuff accompanies your drinks. The young staff are not the types to over-charge, but at other bars on this calle they might, so make this your stop if you need a break from the crowds in this area.

Vitae
Calle Sant'Antonio 4118

Open: M - Sat, 9 a.m. - 1:30 a.m.

To get there: From Campo San Luca, walk towards Accademia, the bar is in a calle to the right.

Sit at metal tables outside this very popular bar and order an actual cocktail instead of wine or coffee. They make an excellent Spritz, and drinks are accompanied by bowls of peanuts. An excellent assortment of *tramezzini* and other snacks are offered, and as an added bonus, the bar is open late. It can be hard to find a table after 9 p.m.

Devils Forest
Calle Stagneri 5185

Open: Daily, 10 a.m. - 1 a.m.

To get there: From the Rialto Bridge, walk into Campo San Bartolomeo and go right. Calle Stagneri and the bar are on your left.

Late nighters are bound to run across this popular pub at some point. They are open late and are usually packed. Irish beer, backgammon and soccer are the focal points. As a tourist, you will pay a higher price than a local. A changing daily lunch menu is reasonable and good. Since it is an English style pub, they speak English, if brusquely.

Bacaro Jazz
Salizada del Fontego dei Tedeschi 5546

Open: Th - T, 4 p.m. - 3 a.m.

To get there: From the Rialto Bridge, walk into Campo San Bartolomeo and make a left onto Salizada del Fontego dei Tedeschi. The bar will be on your right.

There is no way to miss Bacaro Jazz with those brightly colored flashing lights outside. A very expensive – by Venetian standards – place to hang out, but the staff knows where their paycheck comes from, and they are very friendly to tourists. Prices are well marked so you know what you are getting into. Bacaro serves overpriced, substandard food too. So why go? To hang out with other tourists and talk in a place where you feel comfortable. The jazz soundtrack doesn't hurt, either.

Harry's Bar
Calle Vallaresso 1323

Open: Every day, midday to midnight

To get there: From Piazza San Marco, walk away from the Basilica and through the exit on the left. Make a left on Calle Vallaresso. The bar will be all the way down and on your left.

It's famous, it's expensive, and it should be checked out at least once, if only for a drink. The white-coated bartenders are institutions and are incredibly cool guys. There is something special about a bartender who treats everyone the same, whether they are in furs or jeans, especially in a place like Harry's. They seem to know that the next Hemingway might be dressed in a dirty T-shirt. To experience Harry's on the cheap, go in the afternoon or before the dinner hour, sit at the bar, and order a coffee or Prosecco (Prosecco – NOT champagne!) This won't set you back more than 7 Euro. If you can afford to spend a little more, try a tiny glass of the world famous Bellini cocktail – Prosecco and fresh white peach juice (14 Euro) – or a perfect ice cold martini (15 Euro). Do it once, and love it or hate it, but you'll be able to say you sat on the same barstool Hemingway did.

~~~~~~

One winter afternoon, I stopped into Harry's to buy a Bellini, because I was flush, and needed to break a large banknote. Harry's was empty except for a table of Germans drinking tea, three waiters doing their after-lunch counting, the bartender, and me. I was sitting at the bar in my happy little world when in walks a young woman with a backpack, dressed like she was headed to a Grateful Dead concert. She clearly only wanted to use the restroom but was quickly herded into a seat by one of the waiters. They handed her a menu, and I watched her eyes get round as saucers as she read it. "I only want a tea," she said, very quietly and with a frightened look on her face. Then she went off to the restroom.

They served her the tea, and of course it looked fabulous.

I summoned the bartender, and said, very secretively, "I would like to buy that girl her tea." He looked at me as though I wanted to murder her or something. His eyes got as wide as hers did when she looked at the menu. "Why?" he asked me. "Because I just want to." I told him. "Do you want me to tell her you are buying her tea?" "No," I said. "But just don't charge her again after I leave!" The bartender was stunned that I would do this for a stranger with no ulterior motive. He said under his breath so only the waiters and I could hear him, "She wants to buy that girl her tea!" The three waiters all looked at me, eyes wide.

When the bartender brought me the bill, he said "Since YOU are buying the tea, I am giving you a very good price." It was four dollars or something, and I left without saying anything to the girl, and when I go to Harry's now, occasionally a second Prosecco shows up out of nowhere. It's karma, man. - S.E.

~~~~~~

L'Olandese Volante
Campo San Lio 5658

Open: M - Thr, 11 a.m. - 12:30 a.m., Fri - Sat, 11 a.m. - 2 a.m, Sun 5 p.m. to 12:30 a.m.

To get there: The bar is in Campo San Lio

Cozy and warm inside during cold months and lively and colorful outside in warm months, L'Olandese is one place to see and be seen by a young Venetian crowd and tourists from many nations. The bandana-wearing staff are friendly and speak some English. It is rare to be overcharged here, although a carafe of wine or a tall Guinness might cost you 50 cents more or less depending on who is ringing you up. The Spritz are excellent, and come with bowls of popcorn during Spritz hour. A selection of sandwiches and salads are served, but the best thing to order is a big bowl of French Fries, especially when you need a late night snack.

$\sim\sim\sim\sim\sim\sim\sim\sim\sim\sim\sim\sim\sim\sim\sim\sim\sim\sim\sim\sim\sim\sim\sim\sim\sim\sim\sim\sim\sim\sim\sim\sim\sim\sim\sim\sim\sim\sim\sim$

At the Accademia Museum, there is a 600-year-old painting by Giovanni Mansueti, "Miracle of the Relic of the Holy Cross in Campo San Lio." If you go to the Accademia, take a good look at this painting, then go stand in Campo San Lio, facing L'Olandese Volante. You will see that the façade of the building is the same now as it was when the picture was painted. Some strange iridescent tiles over the top of the bar are still there today.

On my second trip to Venice, when I was stunned and elated by everything I saw, I stood in the doorway of the church in Campo San Lio to take shelter from a sudden rainstorm, it being too late to go into L'Olandese Volante. The next day, I went to the Accademia for the first time, saw the painting, and realized I had been standing the night before in the exact spot as the 600-year-old priest who was looking back at me from the painting. I felt a connection with that priest and I have had a connection with Campo San Lio ever since. If you sit at L'Olandese Volante's outdoor tables on a hot, still summer afternoon, you can look up and almost see the ghosts of beautifully dressed 15th century women in the windows above. - S.E.

~~~~~~

Wine Bar Angio
Ponte della Venezia Marina 2142

Open: W - M, 7 a.m. to Midnight

To get there: Walk down Riva degli Schiavoni to Riva San Biagio. You will see the metal chairs of the café on the left.

Stop for a glass of wine or a cup of coffee over the bridge on the Riva degli Schiavoni, and you will pay too much for too little. Just cross one more bridge and sit down at one of the metal tables at this cool bar, and you will have an even more fantastic view of the Lagoon than you do down on the Riva degli Schiavoni. A number of good wines by the glass are offered, and if you expect to have more than one (which you may with this view), go ahead and order a bottle. A perfect Spritz, Guinness on tap, espresso drinks and a selection of fine teas are offered, and for food, the little *panini* are great. Gelato concoctions are offered from the *gelateria* next door.

Da Bacco
Salizzada San Provolo 4620

Open: Th - T, 9 a.m. - Midnight

To get there: From Piazza San Marco, walk to the left of the Basilica and make a right at the canal, go over the bridge onto Ruga G. Apollonia. Walk straight to Calle delle Rasse. Go to the bar on the left corner of Calle delle Rasse – **not** the green tinted bar on the right.

This is a tricky area to navigate when it comes to honest bars. Thankfully, there is Da Bacco, which offers a selection of good wines by the glass and delicious, housemade *tramezzini* and *panini*. You can eat standing at the bar where you will be rubbing elbows with gondoliers or have them bring your sandwiches to small wooden tables. The couple who run the place are a bit chilly, but won't overcharge you.

Zanzibar
Campo Santa Maria Formosa

Open: M - Sat, 9 a.m. - 1 a.m.

To get there: The bar is in Campo Santa Maria Formosa. Look for the tiny red hut on the canal.

Tables are set up outside this bar on the canal between two major thoroughfares (one to Piazza San Marco, one to Rialto) because the inside is too small to fit anybody. Even with the constant stream of people, Zanzibar is a calm and tranquil place. Lots of Venetians read the paper here or meet friends for Spritz at night, and some sit here all day long, getting up only when a customer stops at their newsstand or clothing store a few feet away. Not much in the way of food is offered, but they have decent wine and beer, good coffee and Spritz, and gelato. They are open very late and the staff of young men is efficient and friendly. On warm, moonlit nights, the place is heavenly.

Inishark	***Open:*** T - Sun, 6 p.m. - 1:30 a.m.
Calle Mondo Nuovo 5787	

To get there: From Campo Santa Maria Formosa, walk towards Rialto down Calle Mondo Nuovo. The bar will be on your right.

This bar has a real bar! One that you can sit at! It is open only in the evenings, and is very popular with British and Irish tourists as well as with the locals. Lots of beer and decent wine from a bottle, not a tap, are what you get here. There are good sandwiches too, or maybe those grilled toast and cheese things just taste better when you have had a few drinks. If there is a soccer game on, you might not be able to get in the door. Occasionally a band traveling through Italy will get a gig here, and it can be fun if you happen to be in Inishark when they do. All events – well, just soccer or bands – are posted outside in front, so when you see the sign for Inishark (and believe me you will know it when you see it) stop and see what's going on. If there is a big soccer match on TV, they might open during the day for it, but only go if you are really into soccer.

La Cantina Wine Bar
Campo San Felice 3689

Open: M - Sat, 10 a.m. - 10 p.m.
T - Sat in winter.

To get there: From Campo Santi Apostoli, walk down Strada Nova and cross the first bridge to Campo San Felice. The bar will be on your left.

In a tiny campo right off Strada Nova is this wonderful wine bar run by two lively young guys, Francesco and Andrea, who really love what they do. They offer a fine selection of wines by the bottle or glass, all hand-picked and explained in detail, in Italian, by Francesco. Andrea speaks more English and can help you choose if you are unfamiliar with Italian wines. Francesco is the man behind the food bar, and it only takes one look at his work area to see what care and love he puts into what he creates to go with his wines. He makes a fantastic *pasta e fagioli*, creative cheese plates incorporating local fruits, honeys, and *mostardi* (fruit mustards), good sandwiches, and a delicious, ever-changing variety of tiny *crostini*; a tiny quail's egg on a tiny toast, ham with mustard, or smoked fish are some of the offerings you might try. You can sit inside and watch the flow of Venetians who come to the bar for their hourly *ombra* or espresso, or sit outside in good weather and watch the street life of Strada Nova, one of the busiest streets in town. La Cantina has a large selection of French Champagnes in addition to the ever-changing selection of Italian wines.

Vecia Carbonera
Rio Terra della Maddelena 2329

Open: T - Sun, 10 a.m. - 11 p.m.

To get there: Find Campo d. Maddelena on your map; the bar is near the canal and bridge.

Located on a very crowded stretch of the main thoroughfare between the train station and Rialto, this wine bar is a tranquil place to get away from the crowds, hide, write, read, or have a clandestine affair. Order your wine at the bar and walk into the back room, full of big wooden tables overlooking a canal. The wines are good, inexpensive, and served up by a hip staff. The ancient stereo plays selections of jazz, blues, and Latin music, and occasionally static. Vecia Carbonera's snacks are just passable – the *crostini* and *panini* generally taste as though they have been sitting around for awhile. On Thursday and Sunday nights they have live music, usually jazz. Their hours tend to be a little erratic, but if they are closed, check out La Cantina, up the street, instead.

Fiddler's Elbow
Corte dei Pali 3847

Open: Th - T, 5 p.m. - Midnight

To get there: From Campo Santi Apostoli, walk down Strada Nova. Keep to the right of the street, and after a few blocks look for a small campo. The bar is in this campo on the right. If you get to the first bridge, you have gone too far.

Great music, such as U2, the Doors, and Radiohead is played loudly at this fun Irish pub. There is always someone behind the bar who speaks perfect English for those evenings when you just want to be understood. Lots of good beer on tap, cocktails, and passable wine are offered. Sometimes there are tables outside in the campo.

Nova Vita	***Open:*** M - Th, 9 a.m. - Midnight
Strada Nova 4000	F - Sat 9 a.m. - 2 a.m.

To get there: From Campo Santi Apostoli, go past the San Sofia Traghetto stop and it is the first bar on the left, with a few tables in front with very colorful cloths.

Run by a super-friendly staff, this is THE place to stop for *tramezzini* and Spritz on Strada Nova. You will have to come twice; around noon for the *tramezzini,* and in the evening for Spritz. The *tramezzini* sell out quickly. If you don't make it in time simply order one of the tasty *panini* or a slice of *"rustica"* (like quiche) instead. Nova Vita's Spritz is one of the best and cheapest in town, and as an added bonus they are open till 2:00 a.m. on the weekends.

Maitardi Enobar	***Open:*** M - Sat 9:30 a.m. - 10:00 p.m.
Campiello Corner 5600	Daily 9:30 a.m. - 11:30 p.m. in summer

To get there: the bar is in the tiny but busy Campiello Corner. Look for the awning that says "Enobar."

Campiello Corner is smack dab in the thoroughfare between Rialto and both the train station and the S.S. Giovanni & Paolo area - a crossroads – but there was never anyplace good to hang out there. Until now! Maitardi seems unassuming from the outside, but they offer some very interesting wines by the glass, as well as a very drinkable house wine, some great cheeses and other snacks, and a wonderful vantage point for some serious people watching. They offer flights and a weekly bottle special. The bar itself is tiny, but the outdoor tables are perfect for hanging out and watching the constant stream of locals and tourists.

Un Mondo di Vino
Salizzada San Canciano 5984/A

Open: T - Sun, 10 a.m. - 3:00 p.m., and 5:15 p.m. - 10 p.m.

To get there: From Campo Santa Maria Nova, walk towards down Salizzada San Canciano towards Rialto. The bar will be on your left.

This small and somewhat cramped bar has an exceptional list of wines by the glass and a plethora of tasty treats to go along with the wines. There are various marinated vegetables, more than one kind of *baccalà*, meatballs in tomato sauce, mussels on the half shell – in other words, something for everyone - and it is all so beautifully displayed you'll want to try everything. The young staff are very sweet and accommodating.

Osteria Al Ponte
Calle Larga G. Gallina 6378

Open: M - Sat, 8 a.m. - 9 p.m.

To get there: From Campo San Giovanni e Paolo, cross the bridge. The bar is on the other side.

Overlooking the immense church of S.S. Giovanni e Paolo and the campo surrounding it, this is not so much an osteria as a place to toss back a small glass of extremely inexpensive wine or a *caffé corretto*, and to munch on a selection of tiny, tasty *panini*. This is the kind of bar that steams up inside when it is raining. Try to snag the table by the canal, order a carafe of wine and some sandwiches, and kick back and watch about fifty Venetians come in, drink a glass of wine in one gulp, and talk to each other in a language you could never hope to understand (Venetian, slurred).

Tortuga Pub
Salizzada di Specchieri 4888C

Open: T - Sun, 9 a.m. - 1 a.m.

To get there: At Fondamente Nove, walk to the left up the lagoon till you reach Salizzada di Specchieri. The bar will be on your right.

Chances are that you will never, ever be in this part of town at night unless you are staying around here or are lost. But for night-owls who love their rock music on the metal side, this is a pretty cool place to hang out. The kitchen serves hot sandwiches and salads late into the night, and a good selection of wine and beer is offered. Just remember to bring your map for when you have to find your way home at 2 a.m.

Paradiso Perduto
Fondamenta Misercordia 2539

Open: T - Sun, 11:30 a.m. - 3:30 p.m. and 7:30 p.m. - 1 a.m.

To get there: From Ca' D'Oro, make a left on Strada Nova to Campo San Felice. Make a right up Fondamenta Chiesa, continue on Fondamenta San Felice, left on Misercordia, Paradiso Perduto will be on your right.

This is a crowded, cultural center for the Cannaregio in-crowd. The food is good, the wine is almost free, and sometimes there is live music. The outside tables are a great place to relax during or after sightseeing.

Ai Promessi Sposi
Calle dell'Oca 4367

Open: Th - T, 9 a.m. - 3:15 p.m. and 5:30 p.m. - 11 p.m.

To get there: From Campo Santi Apostoli, walk to the right of the church and make a left on Calle dell'Oca. Ai Promessi Sposi will be on your left.

This osteria on a calle behind Strada Nova offers one of the tastiest selections of *cichetti* in Venice. The bar is tiny, the selection of *cichetti* large, and the wine good and cheap. You can sit in the dining room and order from a regular menu, but it is more fun to stand at the bar with the locals.

Algiubagio
Fondamente Nove 5039

Open: W - M. 6:30 a.m. - 11:30 p.m.

To get there: The bar is on the Fondamente Nove near the Rio d. Gesuiti.

On the Northern edge of the city, Algiubagio has a wonderful floating patio and a view of the cemetery island of San Michele, Murano, and the lagoon. You can't go wrong with one of their homemade pizzas, a plate of pasta or one of the many unique and tasty *tramezzini*. They also have one of the best Spritz in town. Order a half-liter of wine and kick back to watch the speedboats race for awhile. A new dining room has recently opened at Algiubagio, and a large selection of wines by the glass is now offered.

Bar Ai Nomboli
Rio Terà dei Nomboli 2717C

Open: M - F, 7 a.m. - 8 p.m.

To get there: From Campo San Polo, walk with the church on your right to Calle Saoneri. Follow Calle Saoneri to Rio Terà dei Nomboli.

This bar offers good espresso and other morning beverages as well as a small assortment of croissants and brioche. In mild weather there are outside tables under an awning. Despite its good coffee, Nomboli is most famous for its selection of sandwiches, listed on wood plaques on the wall. In back of the bar there are bottles of liquor, aperitifs and liqueurs and it is not uncommon if you roll in for a coffee during mid-to-late morning to see some workmen enjoying an *ombra* or something stronger. Most people buy the sandwiches to take-out. Although not much English is spoken here, the owners are friendly.

SAN POLO

Bancogiro
Campo San Giacometto 122

Open: T - Sun, 10:30 a.m. - 3 p.m.
T - Sat, 6:30 p.m. - Midnight

To get there: The front entrance of Bancogiro is in Campo San Giacometto

Cruising down the Grand Canal in a vaporetto, you will pass by the out-door dining area of Bancogiro, a few wooden picnic tables right on the Canal. It looks expensive, but it is not. Come right at 6:30 p.m., buy a carafe of wine, and you can sit outside at the tables and enjoy that view for a fraction of what it would cost at the Lowenbrau bar on the other side of the bridge. You might have to give up your seat at 8 p.m. when the dinner crowd comes, but you can also reserve yourself a table. The food is excellent.

Ciak 1
Campiello San Tomà 2807

Open: Daily, 7 a.m. - 9 p.m.

To get there: From Campo San Tomà, walk towards Rialto. The bar is in the Campiello San Tomà.

This place is larger than it looks. There is a huge bar inside at which you may stand to drink your coffee, juice or other drinks. There are booths with leather banquettes and even a back room with more seating. They have a good assortment of pastries to consume with your morning coffee. The flaky almond twists are heavenly. By late morning, snacks are coming out of the kitchen, and fresh sandwiches are stacked on the bar. They are available for eating there or for take out. The bar also has nice wines by the glass, sometimes served with little *crostini*. The paranoid, cautious or arithmetically challenged will be pleased to know there is no possibility of ever being overcharged because the bar's checks are computerized. In warm weather there is outside seating in the campiello.

Ruga Rialto
Vecchia San Giovanni 692

Open: T - Sun, 11 a.m. - 2:30 p.m. and 6 p.m. - 1 a.m.

To get there: From the Rialto Bridge, walk up the Ruga d. Orefici. Make the first left. The bar will be a few streets down on your left.

There are only a few stools and not much room to move around here, but that is not a deterrent to the dozens of Venetians who make Ruga Rialto a stop on their nightly bar crawl. A number of great wines by the glass are offered as well as good Spritz, beer and espresso. Some *cichetti* are offered; a large plate of thinly sliced salami, accompanied by breadsticks, tastes pretty great late at night. In the back are two large dining rooms where big plates of Venetian specialties are offered.

Muro
Campo Bella Vienna 222

Open: M - Sat 8:00 a.m. - 3:00 p.m. . and 5:00 p.m. - 1:00 a.m.

To get there: From the Rialto Bridge, walk up Ruga de Orefici to Vecchia San Giovanni and make a right. The bar will be on your left as you enter the Campo.

This is one of the cool, hip bars that is changing the landscape of the Venetian night. Inside, there is a very modern, almost "Clockwork Orange" theme; outside, people stand in large clumps drinking wine in the campo. There are lots of wines by the glass, good grappas, and loud house music. In other words: a lot of fun, especially late at night. The restaurant has views of the campo and an eclectic, slightly pricey menu.

Al Marca	***Open:*** M - Sat 9:00 a.m. - 3:00 p.m.
Campo Bella Vienna 213	and 6:00 p.m. - 9:30 p.m.

To get there: From the Rialto Bridge, walk up Ruga de Orefici to Vecchia San Giovanni and make a right. The bar will be on your right as you enter the Campo.

A visit to the fish market is not complete without standing alongside shoppers and locals in the campo and sipping a coffee or Spritz at Al Marca. There is no indoor seating, and just a couple of benches outside, but who needs a seat when the setting is so much fun? There is a list of wines by the glass, served in nice stemware, and *panini* to munch on if you are hungry. There is nothing more glorious on a beautiful Saturday morning in Venice, than an 11:30 a.m. Spritz at Al Marca.

L' Archivio	***Open:*** 7:30 a.m. - 9:00 p.m. daily
Fondamenta dei Frari 2565	

To get there: the bar is across the canal from the front of the Frari church.

The name L'Archivio is a reference to the Archives of State, which are across the canal in a building that runs along the side of the Frari church, and the bar is an excellent stop for a snack or a quick, inexpensive lunch. You may sit down to eat, or take your selections with you. If you eat at L'Archivio, you place your order at the counter, find a table, and your food is delivered to your table on a round wooden serving dish. The *tramezzini* here are excellent; the bread is fresh, and the fillings well balanced and delicious. The *tramezzini* made with roast pork are especially good.

A varied selection of *cichetti* includes breaded chicken on a skewer and *polpetti*. Both are flavorful and taste freshly made, but they are a little dry perhaps because they are rewarmed. There is also a large assortment of shrimp and fish such as breaded *gamboretti* on a skewer or *baccalà mantecato*, small portions of lasagna, and grilled and marinated vegetables - a good selection of warm and cold treats.

The selection of wines by the glass is impressive and the women who work here are friendly and patient with those who are indecisive about what they want. Most of them speak at least a little English. L'Archivio is a good place to grab lunch on the go or to sit and rest for a while when you are foot weary and hungry or thirsty. You are not only welcome to bring something to read, they provide it for you as well.

Enoteca Vinus Venezia
Dorsoduro 3961

Open: M - Sat, 10 a.m. - Midnight

To get there: Find the corner of San Pantalon and Crosera, and find the unnamed street a couple of streets to the left. The bar will be on your right.

Hidden away on an unnamed street, this new wine bar is sleek and modern, but not uppity. There are only three tables and a long chrome bar, covered with black stone. The tables have handy built-in wine bottle holders. Nine different whites and nine reds are offered by the glass, and there is a large list of bottles for purchase. Mini *panini*, cheeses and cured meat plates are also available.

Café Blue
Calle dei Preti 3778

Open: M - F, 8 a.m. - 2 a.m.
and Sat, 5 p.m. - 2 a.m.

To get there: From the Frari, walk with the church on your right, make a right on Salizada San Rocco, and a left on Calle d. Scuola. After the bridge, the bar will be on your right.

A fun, hip bar, packed with students and locals all day and all night. The owner is always looking for new things to try out on his customers; for instance, they serve afternoon tea and have a large selection of single malt whiskeys. They also have good wines by the glass, Guinness on draught, great house music, and tasty sandwiches, plus some assorted salty things to munch on at the bar. Every night from 8 p.m. to 9 p.m. all drinks are half price. Of course, once they get you in there you may never leave. There is a computer available for customers to check e-mail, for free.

Il Caffé
Campo Santa Margherita 2963

Open: M - Sat, 7:30 a.m. - 2 a.m.

To get there: the bar is in Campo Santa Margherita

This is the daytime and evening in-place for young intellectuals and hipsters. Incredibly cheap wine, coffee and sandwiches are offered. The outside seating area is a wonderful place to get some sun and to eavesdrop on college students.

Ai Do Draghi
Calle della Chiesa 3665

Open: Daily 7:30 a.m. - 2:00 a.m. Apr - Oct.
F- W 7:30 a.m. - 10:00 p.m. Nov - Mar

To get there: the bar is at the top of Campo Santa Margherita, just to the left of the church.

Yet another great bar in Campo Santa Margherita, with plenty of tables outside in the campo in the shade of the bell tower. They serve a great Spritz (possibly the best, and definitely the cheapest, in the campo) and have really tasty sandwiches.

DORSODURO

Marguerite DuChamp
Campo Santa Margherita 3019

Open: Daily, 9 a.m. - 2 a.m.

To get there: The bar is in Campo Santa Margherita

Very hip, very cool and very packed, DuChamp is the most popular bar in Campo Santa Margherita after 9 p.m. Metal tables and chairs outside seem to all be full of young students drinking absolutely nothing. For those who drink it might be one of the large selection of beers, or a Spritz. Wine is cheap and tastes cheap, but they also serve up some of the best coffee in Venice. They have a small selection of sandwiches. During the day, you will have the place to yourself and can watch the lively action in the campo.

Madigan's Pub
Campo Santa Margherita 3053

Open: Th - T, 7:30 a.m. - 2 a.m.

To get there: The bar is in Campo Santa Margherita

Right across from DuChamp, this bar has really good coffee and a nice selection of wine by the glass served in large, crystal wine glasses. There are always tables here, even when DuChamp is packed. Only go if you can sit outside on the campo because the inside is boring and smells like cleaning products.

Cantinone Gia Schiavi/Vini al Bottegon
Fondamenta Maravegie 992

Open: M - Sat, 8 a.m. - 8:30 p.m.; Sun, 8 a.m. - 2 p.m.

To get there: From Accademia, walk to the right onto Calle Gambara, follow it around to the left and follow the canal to the bar which is on the left at the second bridge.

This wine shop serves all the great things a regular bar does, with the constant stream of people that a good bar has. The best time to come here is at lunch to sample some very original and delectable *crostini* – a tuna spread, topped with leeks, or a mild goat cheese, topped with fruit mustard, come to mind. They have a great Spritz and a good sampling of wine by the glass. Sip an *ombra* while looking at the fine wine selection and perhaps choose a bottle to take home. The owner might offer you a glass of *Fragolino*, a local strawberry flavored wine, and then try to sell you a bottle. If you like it, buy it – it is next to impossible to find outside of the Veneto. This is also a great place to buy bottled liquor and liqueurs; they have some of the best prices in town.

Al Prosecco
Campo San Giacomo dell'Orio 1503

Open: M - Sat, 8 a.m. - 10:30 p.m.

To get there: The bar is in Campo San Giacomo dell'Orio

The outdoor metal tables of this excellent bar are a perfect place to hang out and observe Venetian life. During Autumn, the sun hits the bar around noon, and you can usually sit outside comfortably and with perfect light. The citizens of Santa Croce are interesting to watch, old ladies mingling with drunks. The children playing soccer are just a little wilder than those in, say, Campo Santa Margherita. They serve good wines in nice stemware for a very good price. They also make an excellent Spritz. No *tramezzini* are offered, but they do have wonderful *panini* with unusual stuffings such as grilled radicchio and smoked, melted cheese, or *soppressata* with peppery arugula. They have good salads too. You never have to worry about being treated like a tourist here, and the staff is honest and very nice.

Bagolo
Campo San Giacomo dell'Orio 1584

Open: T - Sun, 7 a.m. - 2 a.m.

To get there: The bar is in Campo Giacomo dell'Orio

This new, modern bar has a large, airy inside seating area and wicker chairs outside in the campo; they have good wines by the glass, a great Spritz, and a large selection of interesting grappas. It is very upscale for this area, and more expensive than Al Prosecco, but is a really nice place to sit down with the paper or have a shot of grappa after dinner.

Gelaterie,
Pasticcerie &Other
FOOD SHOPS for the Traveler

There are dozens of pastry shops, delis, grocery stores, and wine shops all over Venice. Here are a few that we like, but get to know the shops around your apartment or hotel, too. Many campi and calli have outdoor fish and vegetable markets – watch for them. Most food shops are open in the morning, close for a long lunch, and reopen at around 3:30 p.m. until 7 p.m. or so. Almost everything is closed Sunday. We have noted shops that are open in the afternoon and on Sundays.

SAN MARCO

Pasticceria Marchini
Spedaria 676

This justifiably famous pastry shop has expensive and delicious cookies, chocolates and nutty, chewy tortes. Their bags of cookies make wonderful gifts for others, if you can stop yourself from opening the bag before you get them home. Try the *pignoli* cookies, little nuggets covered with pine nuts.

Paolin
Campo San Stefano 3464

Paolin has some of the best gelato in Venice, and a few tables in Campo San Stefano at which to enjoy it. The green apple is perfect for a sweltering hot day – not overly sweet, a bit tart, and very refreshing. They also serve a nice Spritz if you aren't in the mood for gelato.

Nave de Oro
Calle Mondo Nuovo 5786

Wine sold from the barrel (into plastic water bottles) or bottle. One liter of wine from the barrel costs around 2 Euro. Bring your own empty bottle, or they will supply one.

Il Laboratorio
C.D. Caffettier 6672

Prepared foods to take out; lasagna, some deep-fried snacks, focaccia, and a pizza oven with fresh pizza. They also have a nice selection of wines by the bottle.

Il Punto Biologico
C.D. Caffettier 6651

A very large and well-stocked natural foods store.

Suve Supermarket

Salizzada San Lio 5811/18

Open: M - Sat, 9 a.m. to 8 p.m. and Sun, 8:45 a.m. - 7:30 p.m.

A small, crowded supermarket, good for staples. For vegetables, go to the vegetable stand across the street on Salizzada San Lio.

Cip Ciap

Calle dell Mondo d. Novo 5799A

Open W - M 9:00 a.m. - 9:00 p.m.

This little shop just off Campo Santa Maria Formosa sells pizza by the slice, little cocktail pizzas, and *torta rustica* – a sort of frittata in a crust. It's a great place to get some snacks for your hotel room or apartment, or to eat at on a bench in the campo.

CANNAREGIO

Mauro El Forner de Canton

Strada Nova 3845 B

A fantastic bakery. The fig bread is to die for, and the flavored breadsticks are very addicting.

Co-op Supermarket

Rio Terra S.S. Apostoli 4612

Not our favorite supermarket, but good in a pinch.

Nave de Oro
Rio Terra S.S. Apostoli 4657

Wine sold from the barrel or bottle. A number of local, fresh varietals are offered straight from the barrel into whatever vessel you supply (if you don't have a vessel, they will supply an empty plastic bottle).

Puppa Roberto
Calle Spezier 4800

This tiny *pasticceria* has good espresso and a delectable assortment of pastries. The puff pastry with hazelnuts is out of this world; there are lots of gooey chocolate and cream filled goodies too. The pastries have the lightness and complexity of the best French pastry while remaining entirely Italian in style and flavor. The shop itself isn't anything special, but the pastries have that special glow that comes from being made by an expert hand.

Billa Supermarket
Strada Nova 3660

A large supermarket with great hours – they are open daily from 8:30 a.m. to 7 p.m.

Rizzo
Rio Terà San Leonardo 1355

This bakery/deli/grocery/wine shop has an excellent selection of basics you need for your apartment or hotel room. It is also a great place to buy food to take home as souvenirs. It looks small in the front, but it is a long cavern with the deli in the back.

Giacomo Rizzo
San Giovanni Crisostomo 5778

This gorgeous shop is filled with exotic pastas and vinegars and other Italian treats, but locals come here to buy international foods such as coconut milk, taco shells, and Betty Crocker brownie mix.

SAN POLO

The best place to shop for food in Venice is the Rialto fish and vegetable market; not only for the outdoor market itself, but also for the butchers, delicatessens, and other food shops that surround it. Shopping there on a warm Saturday morning can be bliss. Please remember that the citizens of Venice are there to buy sustenance, not to snap photos, or to be snapped. Absolutely bring your camera, but don't stand in the way of paying customers to get that perfect shot.

The hours of the fish market are Tuesday through Saturday from 8 a.m. to 1 p.m. Most of the independent shops are open a little later. The vegetable market and some of the surrounding shops are also open on Monday.

Drogheria Mascari
Ruga d. Speziali 381
http://www.imascari.com

In the heart of the Rialto fish and vegetable market area, this family-owned shop is worth a special trip all on its own. This is where locals go when they are looking for an exotic spice, Chinese tea, Tabasco sauce or *Picolit* wine. The staff wear white smocks and lovingly wrap purchases in colorful paper. The wine room is hidden through a doorway in the back of the store and is worth a closer look. Gabriele, the youngest son, speaks English and can help you find an interesting wine or two to take home or back to your room.

Pasticceria Rizzardini
Campiello dei Meloni 1415

Located just a few steps beyond Campo San Polo as you walk towards the Rialto, Rizzardini is a wonderful place for a morning coffee. It is usually crowded, but there is order within the chaos, and it does not take long to get served. Many of the breakfast treats are in self-service cases, so you can order your coffee and then select your own croissant or brioche. The espresso is excellent with a full body flavor and a rich *crema*. This tiny shop has an awesome selection of pastries. There are several different types of croissants as well as *krapfen* and flaky almond buns. It is amazing to see the variety of goodies that come out of such a small workspace, and they are all worth trying. The place works on a sort of honor system; you tell someone behind the counter what you have had, and she will tell you how much you owe. You can also buy pastries *per portare via* – to take away.

Macelleria
Calle Saoneri 2725

Giampietro Fabbro, the handsome white-haired owner of this butcher shop is behind the counter whenever the store is open for business. He carries all varieties of meat, and will cut, slice and pound meat to your order. In addition to delicious and reasonably priced fresh meats he has some prosciutto, sausages, salamis and eggs for sale. All his meat his excellent, but the veal is especially delicate and tender and his chicken especially flavorful. Take your place in front of the counter and wait among the local women for your turn to be served. If you speak even a little Italian you will be rewarded with recipe suggestions from this amiable butcher.

Pasticceria Targa
Ruga Ravano 1068

You can stop in here any time to enjoy a cup of outstanding coffee and wonderful breakfast treats. Richer pastries appear during the day, and special goodies, such as *fritelle* turn up for the appropriate holidays. They also sell candies – the incredibly long licorice whips coiled in the window make this place easy to recognize. Stand-up service only.

Rialto Biocenter
Campo Beccarie 366

This small but well-stocked natural foods store has fresh, organic vegetables and whole grain breads in addition to tofu, juice, organic wines and the like.

Mauro El Forner de Canton
Ruga Vecchia San Giovanni 603

A very good, very crowded bakery with less than amiable salespeople. There is a second store in Cannaregio that is less crowded, has nicer salespeople, and has the same great stuff.

Pavan Marina
Campo San Tomà 2823

This is a tiny shop with delicious fresh baked breads and pastries. They also carry a small number of grocery items such as bottled water and jams. Everything is very fresh here, but get there early. When they sell out, that's it until tomorrow. Locals frequently reserve their favorites ahead of time.

Biga Supermarket
Rio Terà Frari 2605B
Open Sundays and Holidays, shorter hours

This *supermercato* carries everything including meat, deli goods, regular grocery items and produce. You have to wander through narrow aisles and look into alcoves, but this is a very complete little market.

Il Pastaio
Campiello C. Battisti 219

If you like to cook fresh pasta and do not mind a little attitude with your purchase, this is the place for you. The pasta is absolutely first rate. There is a huge assortment of both regular and filled pastas. You might buy some *tagliatelle* made from porcini mushrooms, beets, spinach, whole wheat or even chocolate, or try *tortellini* or *tortelloni* filled with porcini mushrooms, spinach and ricotta, chicken, veal, or an almost endless list of other vegetable and/or meat combinations. The staff is not overly friendly, but they will give you cooking times, and the pasta itself is a treat.

Millevoglie di Tarcisio Gelato

Located in the back of the Frari. Look for the name on the awning. These people love gelato; they understand important decisions such as the placement of scoops on the cone. They carry some soy flavors – usually chocolate and hazelnut. Outside service only; no tables. An attached store sells excellent pizza and *calzone*.

Casa del Parmigiano
Erbaria 214/215
www.aliani-casadelparmigiano.it

You will find this fantastic cheese shop in the Erbaria, just off the fish market. They stock a selection of perfectly ripened cheese from all over Italy, cured meats, olives, and other savory treats. The staff are incredibly nice to both locals and tourists. This is a fabulous place to buy items for your apartment or for an impromptu picnic. It does get a bit crowded at times, but it is worth the wait. Check out their webpage for some great information on cheeses and the other products they carry, as well as recipes.

Aliani Gastronomia
Ruga Vecchia San Giovanni 654/55

Aliani Gastronomia is a food lover's paradise. On one side of Aliani there is a huge counter with an assortment of fresh pasta for sale. On a typical day the selection might include gnocchi, *tortellini Bolognese*, ravioli with porcini mushrooms, ravioli with spinach and ricotta, or even ravioli with turnip. They also have a large selection of cooked foods such as spit-roasted chickens, *vitello tonnato*, whole fish, vegetables, potatoes, and salads. On the other side of the shop there is a wonderful deli with all sorts of hams, salami, cheeses - just about anything you can think of and lots you've never heard of.

In Aliani you make your selection; then you take the slip you are given to the cashier whom you pay. You are given a receipt. When you return this to the counterman or woman, you will receive your purchase neatly packaged and ready to take home. The staff will give precise cooking instructions so your ravioli will come out perfectly.

Vizio Virtù Cioccolateria
Calle de Campaniel 2898/A

It is really fun to look at all the different chocolates in this beautiful shop. Some are filled with traditional fillings such as raspberry and others with more unusual flavorings such as saffron. There are even chocolates called Sherlock Holmes and Sigmund Freud that are tobacco flavored, as well as more tempting flavors and scents such as ginger, amaretto, and raspberry.

Little chocolate bowls filled with assorted chocolates are not only delicious but are served up in a clever presentation. There are also pretty little silk bags containing chocolates - molded chocolate spoons, chocolate animals, chocolate letters and even packages of curls and tiny pastilles for decorating your own cakes.

There are boxes in several sizes which can be filled with the chocolates of your choosing. There are so many wonderful flavors and fillings that selecting a few can be difficult, but Mariangela, the owner, and her assistant are so patient and so helpful, the choosing becomes an adventure. Mugs filled with chocolate make a tasty and yet lasting gift, and there is an interesting assortment of books on chocolate. At one end of the counter is an area in which they serve divinely decadent hot chocolate with mounds of whipped cream and chocolate shavings. And if all this is not tempting enough, there is a huge tasting plate of bits and pieces of chocolate and, of course, the entire place smells heavenly.

Igloo Gelato
Calle della Chiesa just off Campo Santa Margherita

There are no tables or chairs here but you are just steps away from Campo Santa Margherita with its many strategically placed benches. Constantly moving foot traffic insures that your gelato or sorbetto will be truly fresh and for the dairy challenged they have one or two flavors of *soia* every day.

Causin
Campo Santa Margherita 2996

This is one of the oldest and most famous *gelaterie* in Venice. They have a large selection of both gelato and *sorbetto* as well as espresso. There are tables inside for savoring your gelato, and a restroom for customer use only.

Billa
Fondamenta Zattere 1491

This supermarket is sort of out of the way, but good if you are staying in this neck of the woods. It is a large, well-stocked store mostly frequented by Venetians.

Tonolo
San Pantalon 3764

How can you not love a pastry shop with poetry on its walls! On the left wall there is a long counter filled with delectable sweet treats. In addition to buying individual sized treats there are whole cakes, and an entire refrigerated case filled with frozen and whipped cream delicacies. The espresso machine is huge and can turn out 8 or 10 cups of heavenly coffee at a time. Service here is prompt and pleasant, but no one is rushed. It is as if everyone understands the importance of deciding between cream puffs filled with *zabaglione* or chocolate, a mousse of *lampone* or *fragole*, or a cake made with almond or mocha cream. If espresso or cappuccino is not your beverage, there is hot chocolate, tea, and an assortment of fresh fruits ready to be turned into juice on request. In the morning you can choose warm, flaky almond pastries, croissants filled with jam or cream, or whole-wheat croissants filled with blueberry preserves, often still warm from the oven. Later in the day there are apricot pastries, apple strudel, giant macaroons and meringues, tiny individual mousses, and a yummy assortment of cakes. Everything here is luscious and no matter what you choose you will be in for a treat, but somehow that knowledge never makes the act of selecting any easier.

SANTA CROCE

Co-op Market
Campo San Giacomo dell'Orio

You won't see any tourists at this market, and you will be able to find just about anything you need. Afterwards treat yourself to a glass of wine at Al Prosecco next door.

Our favorite non-food shops AND resources FOR THE traveler IN Venice

A great resource for travelers to all destinations, but especially to Italy, is Slow Travelers **www.slowtrav.com**. There are hundreds of vacation rental listings and reviews, hotel reviews, restaurant reviews, information on how to operate Italian washing machines, hints to help you cope with driving in Italy, plus much more. They also have a great message board - Slow Talk **www.slowtalk.com.**

Bed & Breakfast Corte 1321, *in San Polo*, has accommodations good for larger parties, singles, or couples who like an apartment atmosphere, but also like to have the owners around. There are two suites (one sleeps four, one sleeps six), a double, and a single; all have bathrooms. Additionally, there is a studio apartment on the ground floor that can sleep four and has a bathroom and kitchen. Breakfast is served in the rooms or in a lovely courtyard in warm weather. Corte 1321 has become very popular, so early booking in peak seasons is essential.

For more information, e-mail: *Amelia Bonvini at info@corte1321.com, call: 39-041-522-4923, or visit* www.corte1321.com.

Shopping

Il Pavone
Fondamenta Venier dai Leoni 721, **Dorsoduro**

There are dozens of marbled paper and stationery stores in Venice, but this is one of our favorites. They have lovely writing paper, journals, even ties and aprons with patterns of Venice. The prices are very good, too.

Ottica Caporin
Green Vision
Crosera S. Pantalon 3813, **Dorsoduro**
Tel: *041-523-6883*
Open: M – Sat

Whether you want to treat yourself to Italian sunglasses or frames and lenses or stop in for a quick repair on your glasses, you will not find a friendlier and more helpful group than those who staff this Venice outpost of Green Vision. There is a wide selection of sunglasses as well as an enormous choice of frames. Prescriptions for eyeglasses are international and you might find just what you are looking for here. New glasses are usually ready in about a week, and repairs are often made on the spot or in a day or two. Since the Dolomites, just outside of Venice, are the center of the Italian eyeglass industry, you will be delighted by the prices here. English speakers are welcomed, and you are virtually guaranteed to leave here not only seeing better but smiling.

Italo Chiarion, Artist

If you are looking for watercolors of Venice, try to seek out Italo Chiarion. He is usually on the Molo San Marco after 3 p.m., in front of the gardens, near Harry's Bar and the tourist office. He speaks perfect English and his watercolors are exceptional.

I Vetri a Lume di Amadi
Calle Saoneri 2747, **San Polo**
Tel: 041-523-8089

Located on the right as you walk from San Tomà to San Polo, this tiny glass shop sells only figures of insects, birds, animals and flowers, fruit and vegetables. All of these amazing replicas are made on the premises. You can carry home a tiny treasure by buying an asparagus stalk, a small cat, a scorpion or a bit of coral. The art found in this shop is a far cry from the mass produced souvenirs sold in the tourist shops. Prices vary reflecting the amount of work that goes into each piece. It is worth stopping in just to look at the not-for-sale-fantasy horses in the glass case on the wall. They are so breathtakingly beautiful and delicate that it is difficult to believe they were made by human hands, but you can meet the maker and shake his hand when you have caught your breath.

La Bottega dei Mascareri
Shop - San Polo 80, (Rialto Bridge)
Tel and Fax: 041-522-3857
Studio & shop - 2720 Calle Saoneri, San Polo
Tel and Fax: 041-524-2887

Sergio and Massimo Boldrin have had a shop at the foot of the Rialto Bridge since 1984. The windows, walls and ceilings of this tiny store are jammed with an incredible assortment of handmade masks ranging from the basic *Bauta* in white, gold or black to the small oval *moretta* worn by ladies to replicas of traditional Commedia dell'Arte masks. There are also spectacular Bacchus faces, jesters, suns, moons and leaves, as well as cats, wolves and other animals available. In the Studio and shop on the Calle Saoneri, you can sometimes catch Sergio, Massimo or Rita Perinello at work creating new masks. In addition to the many masks already mentioned you can find wonderful masks replicating Vincent Van Gogh and the Beatles. There are also fanciful Carnival prints and posters painted by Rita. Their masks are unique, especially in their flexibility which makes them more comfortable to wear and much less breakable. Sergio, Massimo and Rita all speak excellent English and enjoy meeting and chatting with Americans and other foreign travelers. No trip to Venice is complete without a trip to a mask shop, so stop by and say "Hi" to the Boldrins for us.

Karisma
Calle Saoneri at Rio Terà dei Nomboli, **San Polo**

This pricey but appealing paper shop has windows filled with unusual and beautiful paper covered items and related objects. There is a lovely collections of seals and wax, and also glass calligraphy pens and ink. The shelves are filled with sketchbooks, address books, diaries, souvenir and photo albums all covered in different papers. For a small gift check out the pretty note paper or book marks, the handmade book plates and tiny address books, The owner spends long hours in his shop and speaks fluent English. He is friendly and helpful and will gladly assist you in finding the perfect gift or leave you free to browse on your own.

Sabbie e Nebbie
Calle Nomboli 2768/A, San Polo
Open: *M - Sat 10:00 a.m. - 12:30 p.m. and 4:00 p.m. -7:30 p.m.*

MariaTeresa Laghi has an assortment of shimmering Asian silks, beautiful ceramics and sumptuous Italian leather goods in her beautiful shop. Fluent in English as well as French and German, she has a wonderful eye for color and will help you find the exact shade or combination of shades of silk scarves that will best suit you. Friendly, helpful and endlessly patient, she makes shopping in Sabbie e Nebbie an enjoyable and rewarding experience.

Hair Technart Salon
Calle dei Saoneri 2719, **San Polo**
Tel: *041-716-765*
Open: *M - Sat 9:30 a.m. - 6:30 p.m.*

The wild and crazy window may fascinate you, but do not let it scare you. Salvo and Miky are consummate professionals, and you will leave their salon looking and feeling better than you did when you entered. Both men are delightfully user friendly and speak enough English to get the job done, so don't fret about getting fuschia hair when you really want blond (or vice versa.)

Mazzon Le Borse
Pelletteria Artigiana
Campiello San Tomà 2807, **San Polo**
Open: *M - Sat*

To get there: The Campiello San Tomà is just off the Campo San Tomà in the direction of the Rialto.

There are dozens if not hundreds of small leather good shops in Venice, but not all feature locally made items at reasonable prices. Mazzon offers both men's and women's wallet and belts. Belts can be cut to your size while you wait. Wallets and change purses are reasonably priced and are available in a variety of leathers and colors. There is a nice selection of purses and shoulder bags also in a variety of styles and leathers. Any bag can be made to order in any leather or color, but it does take three weeks and they do not ship. In the winter there are many shades of brown, black and other darker colors; in the spring, the beautiful pastel leathers make an eye-catching display that is hard to resist.

Il Nido delle Cicogne
Campiello San Tomà 2806, **San Polo**

To get there: The Campiello San Tomà is just off the Campo San Tomà in the direction of the Rialto.

The "Storks' Nest" is a store that a grandmother, aunt, or godmother will not be able to resist. The children's clothes - especially those for infants and toddlers - are exquisite. They are made from the finest and softest fabrics, and sewn with the finest stitches. Although they carry clothes for older children and often feature American and British clothing lines, look for anything made by "Il Gufo" if you want Italian baby clothes that will make you reach for that credit card. The staff here prefers to show you items; they do not really like you looking on your own, but they are endlessly patient about showing you outfits in different colors, styles and sizes. The beautiful clothing is definitely pricey, but how can a grandma resist?

Glossary

Index

Maps

Glossary of Italian and Venetian Words -

Venetian words are Italicized

a
~~~~~~~~~~~~

acciuga - anchovy
aceto - vinegar
aciugheta - anchovy
acqua - water
acqua minerale - bottled water; "non-gassata" or "naturelle" is still water, "con gas" is with bubbles, "acqua del rubinetto" is tap water
acqua cotta - literally cooked water; usually a thick and hearty vegetable soup served over bread
affettati misti - assorted cold meats
affettato - sliced
affumicato - smoked
agio - garlic
aglio - garlic
agnello - lamb
agnolotti - a filled pasta similar to ravioli
agrodolce - sweet and sour
agrume - citrus (usually used in reference to a sauce)
albergo - hotel
albicocca - apricot
al burro e salvia - a pasta sauce made with butter and sage
al cartoccio - baked in parchment paper or foil
al dente- firm; not over-cooked
al forno - baked
alice - fresh anchovy
alla brace - charcoal grilled
alla griglia - grilled
all' arrabbiata - Italian for angry, it refers to a spicy tomato sauce made with chiles and pancetta.
al sangue - rare
al sugo - a simple tomato sauce
altana - wooden roof terraces on Venetian houses
al vapore - steamed
amarena - black cherry – often found in conjunction with gelato (ice cream).
amaretti - small crisp macaroon cookies

amatriciana - a sauce made with pancetta or sausage, hot peppers tomato and onions
amolo - plum
analcolico - non alcoholic drink; bibite analcolica - soft drink
ananas - pineapple
anara - duck
aneto - dill
anguilla - eel
anitra - duck
a puntino - medium
arachidi - peanuts
aragosta - lobster
arancia - orange
arborio - short grained rice used for risotto
arrosto - roasted
articiòco - artichoke
asciutto - dry
assaggio - a taste
àstese - lobster
astice - lobster

~~~~~~~~~~~~ **b**

bacalà - dried, salted cod
bacalà mantecà - dried and salted cod, boiled, then whipped with garlic flavored oil and parsley until it is light and creamy
bàcaro - a tavern
baccalà - salted cod
bagìgi - peanuts
barbabietola - beet
bavette - long narrow pasta
Bel Paese - soft mild cheese
ben cotto - well done
besciamella - bechamel sauce
bevanda - drink, beverage
bianco - white
bibita - drink
bicchiere - glass
bigoli - coarse spaghetti made from whole wheat flour often served with a sauce made with sauteed onions and anchovies
birra - beer, ale

birra alla spina - draught beer
birra chiara - lager
birra in bottiglia - bottled beer
birra scura - stout
bisàto - eel
biscotti - hard cookies - the name means twice cooked
bisi - peas
bistecca - steak
boccia - bowl;
boccia da vino - carafe of wine
bollito - boiled, especially beef
Bolognese - in the style of Bologna; pasta alla Bolognese-with a meat and tomato sauce
borlotti - kidney or cranberry beans
bòsega - grey mullet
bottiglia - bottle
bovoleti - small field snails served with garlic and parsley as cichetti
braciola - chop; di maile - pork chop; di vitello - veal chop
branzino - sea bass
brasato - braised
Bresaola - air dried beef
briciola - crumb
briosca - croissant
brodo- stock; brodo di manzo - beef broth; brodo ristretto - consomme; brodetto - light broth
bruciato - burnt
bruscandoli - wild hop sprouts from Friuli
bruschetta - toasted slice of bread topped with garlic, oil and tomato or other toppings
bucatini - hollow spaghetti
buccia - skin or peel
budino - pudding
bue - beef, ox
butiro - butter

C
~~~~~~~~~~~~~
ca'- house
cacciatore - hunter style - usually means dish contains onions, mushrooms, tomatoes and herbs
caffè - coffee - almost always means espresso

caffè americano - a cup of American style coffee
caffè corretto - espresso with a shot of alcohol
caffè latte - coffee mixed with steamed milk; a latte is just warm milk
caffè lungo - a "long" (weaker) espresso
cappuccino - coffee topped with foamed milk
calle - street
cameriere - waiter
campiello - a small campo
campo - square
canella - cinnamon
canestrèli - scallops
cannocche - mantis shrimp
canoce - mantis shrimp
caparosoli - small clams
caparozzoli - small clams
capatònda - bivavle mollusk
capelonghe - razor clams
cape da deo - razor clams
capesante - scallops
capocuoco - chef ("chef" is also commonly used.)
caragoli - sea snails
carbonara - a sauce with eggs, bacon, cream, and cheese
carciofo - artichoke
cardo - cardoon
carpaccio - thinly sliced raw beef, served with garnishes
carrè -loin; carrè d'agnello - rack of lamb
casolin - grocery store
castagna - chestnut
castrato - mutton
castraùre - tiny spring artichokes
cavolfiore - cauliflower
cavolo - cabbage
cavatappi - corkscrew
cece - chick pea
cetriolo - cucumber
chicco - coffee bean
ciabatta - bread - name means "bedroom slipper" from shape from loaf
cibo - food; cibi precotti - precooked food
cicale di Mare - mantis prawns

cichetti - bite sized bar snacks
ciliegia - cherry
cinghiale - wild boar
cioccolato - chocolate
cipolla - onion
cipolline - onion
clinton - illegal wine made from American grapes
coda di rospa - monkfish
coltello - knife
conchiglia - pasta shaped like a shell
coniglio - rabbit
contorno - side dish such as potatoes or vegetables
coperto - cover charge
cornetto - croissant
corte - courtyard
costoletta - cutlet
cotecchino - pork sausage
cotica - pork rind
croccantini - crunchy caramel and almond bars served like a cookie with sweet wine
crostada - fruit tart
crostini - bread with assorted toppings
crudo - raw
cucchiaino - teaspoon
cucchiaio - tablespoon

d

da portare via - to take out or away
dentice - a fish similar to Red Snapper
diavolo - devil; in regard to food: a spicy red sauce; also alla diavola or fra diavolo
digestivo - an after dinner liqueur
dìndio - turkey
dolce - sweet, dessert
drogheria - grocery store
durelo - chicken gizzard

e

edicola - newstand
enoteca - wine shop

erbe aromatiche - herbs
erba cipollina - chives

fagiano - pheasant
fagioli - dried beans
fagiolini - string beans
faraona - guinea hen
farcite - stuffed
farina - flour
fasiòi - kidney beans
fegato - calf's liver - "alla Veneziana" sliced in long, thin strips and cooked with onions.
fenòcio - fennel
fetta - slice
fettucine - long, flat ribbons of pasta, said to be inspired by Lucretia Borgia's blonde hair
fiaschetteria - wine shop; bar
fico, fichi - fig(s)
figà a la Venexiàna - see fegato
finocchio - fennel
fiori di latte - cream, also a flavor of gelato
fiori di zucchini - zucchini flowers, sometimes deep-fried, or stuffed with cheese
focaccia - flat bread with various toppings
folpetto - a smal octopus
folpi - octopus
forchetta - fork
formaggio - cheese
forno - oven
fragola - strawberry
fragolino - strawberry flavored white wine
frègola - crumb
fritoìn - fried fish stall
frìtole - fritters usually served during Carnivale
frittata - open faced omelet
frittelle - fritters
fritto misto - a mixed fry of seafood, meat, or vegetables
frutta - fruit
frutti di bosco - berries

frutti di mare - "fruits of the sea" - seafood
fugassa - flat bread with various toppings
funghi - mushrooms
fusilli - pasta made in long spirals

g

gambero - shrimp or prawn
garùsoi - sea snails served on toothpicks as a snack
gelato - ice cream
ghiaccio - ice
ghiozzo - goby, a fish
gnocchi - small flour and potato dumplings served as a first course
with sauce
gò - goby, a fish
gotò - glass
granchio - crab
grànso - crab from the Venetian lagoon
gransèola - large Mediterranean crab
granturco - corn or maize
grappa - strong clear brandy made from grapes skin and seeds after juice
has been pressed out for wine
gremolata - a garnish made of minced parsley, lemon peel and garlic
grissini - bread sticks

i

impasto - dough
in camicia - poached
indivia - endive
insalata - salad. May be mista - mixed or verde - green
integrale - whole wheat
involtini - rolled

k

kascher - kosher
khasher - kosher
krapfen - fried doughnut filled with apricot or cream, also kraf

l

lampone - raspberry
latte - milk
latteria - a cheese and dairy store
lattuga - lettuce

lecca lecca - lollypop
lenticchia - lentil
lepre - hare
lesso - boiled - patate lesse are boiled potatoes
lievito - yeast
lievito in polvere - baking powder
lièvaro - hare
limone - lemon
limonata - lemonade
lonza - loin of pork
luccio - pike
lugànega - sausage
lumaca - snail

~~~~~~~~~~~~ m

macedonia - fruit salad
macelleria - butcher shop
maiale - pork
mandorla - almond
mantecato - food stirred until creamy and smooth
manzo - beef
marinara - sauce usually made with tomatoes, onions, garlic and oregano
marmellata - jam (di agrumi - marmalade)
masanète - crabs
mascarpone - double rich cream cheese
mela - apple
melanzana - eggplant
melograno - pomegranate
melone - melon
menta - mint
merluzzo - cod
mezzo - half
miele - honey
milanese - dish associated with Milan
mirtillo - blueberry
minestra - soup containing meat and vegetables
minestrone - a thick soup with meat, vegetables, pasta and beans
misto - mixed
moleche - soft shell crabs
more - blackberry

mortadella - smoked sausage made with beef, pork, fat and seasoning
mostarda - preserves

n
~~~~~~~~~~~~

narànsa - orange
nero - black
nervèti- boiled veal cartilage; served with onion, parsley, oil and vinegar
nocciola - hazelnut
noce - nuts
noce di cocco - coconut
nostrano - homemade locally
novellàme - a mixed fry of sea fish

o
~~~~~~~~~~~~

oca - goose
olio - oil
olive - olives
ombra - a small glass of wine served at a bar
orada - sea bream or gilt head
orata - sea bream
orecchiette - "little ears," small ear-shaped pasta
origano - oregano
ortaggio - vegetable
orto - vegetable garden
orzo - barley
osso - bone
osso buco - braised veal shanks
osteria - local, casual eating establishment or wine bar
ostriche - oysters
ovino - sheep

p
~~~~~~~~~~~~

palombo - shark
pan carrè - sliced bread
pancetta - cured meat resembling un-smoked bacon
pane - bread
pangrattato - bread crumbs
panificio - bakery especially for bread
panini - bread rolls, also sandwiches
panna - cream
panna cotta - custardy dessert

panòcia - corn cob
papavero - poppy seed
pappardelle - wide pasta
Parmigiano - parmesan cheese
parsemolo - parsley
parsuto - ham
passarìn - sole
passeggiata - A very important part of Italian life - the "evening stroll."
Every town has one and everyone is there, talking and checking each
other out.
passera - flounder
passino - sieve or strainer
pasta e fagioli - pasta and bean soup
pasta e fasiòi - pasta and bean soup
pastella - batter
pasticcio - meat, fish, or vegetables mixed with pasta or polenta and baked
pasticceria - pastry shop
pastina - very small pasta used in soups
patata - potato
patate fritte - French fries
patatine - fried potatoes or potato chips
pecorino - hard, sheeps milk cheese
pelato - peeled: pomodori pelati are peeled tomatoes
pentola - large pot
pentolino - saucepan
penne - tubed shaped pasta
peòci -mussels
pepe - pepper
peperoncini - hot peppers
peperoni - (bell) peppers
pera - pear
pesca - peach
pesce - fish
pescespada - swordfish
pesto - paste of oil, basil and pinenuts
petto - breast
peveràda - a condiment served with meats
pezzo - piece
piadina - flat round unleavened bread cooked on a griddle or the hearth

piatto - plate
piccante - spicy
piccata - prepared with butter and lemon
piccione - pigeon
pinoli - pine nuts
pìnsa - cake made with wheat and corn flour, raisins and eggs and other nuts, dried fruits or spices, sold by wieght or by the piece.
piròn - fork
piselli - peas
pizzoccheri - buckwheat pasta
polastro - chicken
polenta - corn meal mush, served as a side dish to meats or sliced and served grilled
polleria - poultry shop
pollo - chicken
polpetta - meatball
polpettone - meatloaf
polpo - octopus
pomo - apple
pomodoro - tomato
pompelmo - grapefruit
porchetta - roast pork
porcini - mushrooms
porro - leek
pranzo - lunch
prezzemolo - parsley
prima colazione - breakfast
primo piatto - first course
profiteroles - dessert of whipped cream or ice cream stuffed cream puffs, covered with chocolate sauce
prosciutto cotto - boiled ham
prosciutto crudo - cured ham
prosecco - white, sparking wine from the Veneto, very popular in Venice
provolone - mild cow's milk cheese
prugna - plum
prugna secca - prune
pùina - ricotta cheese

~~~~~~~~~~~~ q

quaglia - quail
quatro - quarter
quatro stagione - "four seasons." On a pizza, there will be a different topping on each quarter.

~~~~~~~~~~~~ r

radicchio - a purple, bitter vegetable
radicchio di Treviso - perhaps the best radicchio anywhere, milder and crunchier than other Radicchio
radice - radish
rafano - horseradish
ragù - meat sauce
rapa - turnip
rhum - rum
ricetta - recipe
ricevuta - receipt
ricotta - creamy cheese
rigatoni - tubed shaped pasta with ridges
ripieno - stuffed
Risi e Bisi - Venetian dish of rice and peas
riso - rice
risotto - a dish of cooked rice and other ingredients, such as seafood or vegetables
ristorante - upscale eating establishment
rombo - turbot
rosàda - custard made with eggs, sugar and milk
rosmarino - rosemary
rossetti - tiny red mullet
rosso - red
rosticceria - place to buy roasted meats and other foods
rotolo - roll
rucola - arugula, rocket

~~~~~~~~~~~~ s

salsiccia - sausage
sale - salt
salmone - salmon
salsa - sauce
saltimbocca - a veal dish with sage

salumeria - delicatessen
salvia - sage
salvietta - napkin
San Pietro - St. Peter's fish also known as John Dory, Talapia
sarde in saòr - old Venetian dish of sardines marinated with onion, vinegar, pine-nuts and raisins
sarèsa - cherry
scamorza - cow's milk cheese similar to mozzarella, sometimes smoked
scampi - shrimp
schie - small shrimp
sciòso - snail
sciroppo- syrup
scodella - bowl or soup plate
scòrfano - scorpion fish
scotto - scorched
scugèr - spoon
secondo piatto - second course
sedano - celery
sedano rapa - celeriac
segola - onion
senape - mustard
seppie - cuttlefish
servizio - service
sestiere - district
sfògio - sole
sgroppino - after dinner drink of lemon sorbet, vodka and prosecco
sogliola - sole
sopressa - salami from Treviso
sopressata - salami from the Veneto
sorbetto - sorbet
sorgente - a spring
spàreso - asparagus
speck - ham
spicchio d'aglio - clove of garlic
spinaci - spinach
spremuta - fresh fruit juice
Spritz - Venetian aperitif made with white wine and Campari (Spritz bitter) or Aperol (*Spritz con Aperol.*)
spuma - foam or mousse

stinco - shinbone
stoccafisso - dried cod
stracaganàse - dried chestnuts-word means jaw strainers
stracchino - mild, cow milk's cheese from Lombardy
stracotto - pot roast, also overcooked
strutto - lard
stufato - stew
sùca - pumpkin
succo - juice
sugo - juice or gravy
suino - pork
supermercato - supermarket
susina - plum

~~~~~~~~~~~~ t

tacchino - turkey
tagliatelle - long, flat, thin pasta
taleggio - cow's milk cheese from Lombardy, usually aged forty days.
tartina - canapè
tartufi - truffles
tavola - table
tavola calda - "hot table" generally a store with take-out food
tècia - pan or frying pan
tegame - a frying pan or skillet; al tegame – fried
tiramisù - dessert of layered ladyfingers or biscuits, mascarpone cheese, coffee and liqueur
tochèto - small piece
tòcio - sauce
tòco - piece
tòla - table
tonno - tuna
torrone - a type of nougat
torte - cake
tortelli - small ravioli
tortellini - small stuffed pasta
tortelloni - larger stuffed pasta
tortiera - cake pan
tortino - a savory pie
Toscano - from tuscany
tramezzini - small stuffed sandwiches found in many Venetian bars

trattoria - restaurant
triglie - mullet
triglia di scoglio - red mullet
trippa - tripe

u

ubriaco - drunk
uova - egg
uva - grape
uva passa - raisin

v

vapore - steam
vaporetto - water bus
vedelo - calf
verde - green
verdure - vegetable
vermicelli - thin pasta
verza - cabbage
vino - wine
vino di casa - house wine
vino novello - the first wine released from the harvest
vin santo - sweet dessert wine
vitello - veal
vongole veraci - very tiny clams often served in the shell with spaghetti
vovo - egg

w

wurstel - frankfurter

z

zabaion - zabaglione
zabaione - warm custard with sweet wine
zaleto - a type of cookie made with cornmeal and raisins
zampone - a stuffed pig's foot
zenzero - ginger
ziti - wide pasta tubes
zolletta - lump or cube of sugar
zucca - squash
zuccato - a dome shaped dessert
zucchero - sugar
zucchero a velo - confectioners or powdered sugar

zucchero semolato - granulated sugar
zuppa - soup
zuppa inglese - a dessert simliar to English trifle

Alphabetical Listing of Restaurants with corresponding page numbers:

Alphabetical Listing of Bars
with corresponding page numbers:

INDEX

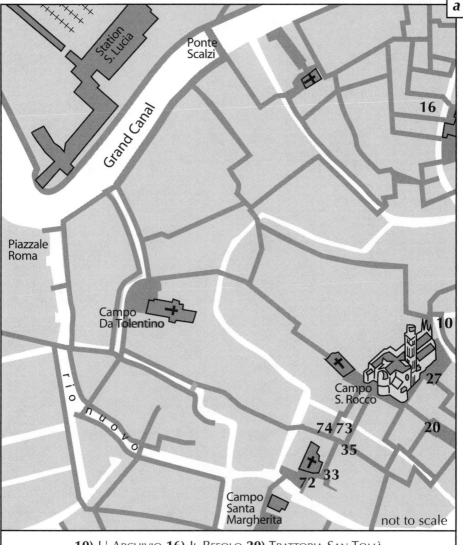

a

Station S. Lucia

Ponte Scalzi

Grand Canal

16

Piazzale Roma

Campo Da Tolentino

rio nuovo

Campo S. Rocco

10

27

20

74 73

35

72 33

Campo Santa Margherita

not to scale

10) L' Archivio **16)** Il Refolo **20)** Trattoria San Tomà
27) La Perla d'Oriente **33)** Da Silvio **35)** Ca' Foscari al Canton
72) Arca **73)** Enoteca Vinus Venezia **74)** Café Blue

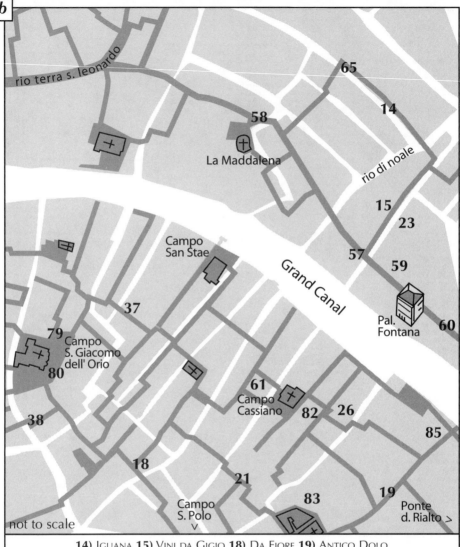

b

rio terra s. leonardo

65

14

58

La Maddalena

rio di noale

15

23

Campo
San Stae

Grand Canal

57

59

37

Pal.
Fontana

60

79

Campo
S. Giacomo
dell' Orio

80

61

Campo
Cassiano

82

26

38

85

18

21

Campo
S. Polo

83

19

not to scale

Ponte
d. Rialto >

14) Iguana **15)** Vini da Gigio **18)** Da Fiore **19)** Antico Dolo
21) Antiche Carampane **23)** Al Fontego dei Pescaori **26)** Poste Vecie
37) La Zucca **38)** Ae Oche **57)** La Cantina **58)** Vecia Carbonera **59)** Fiddler's Elbow
60) Nova Vita **61)** Al Nono Risorto **65)** Paradiso Perduto **79)** Al Prosecco
80) Bagolo **82)** Al Garanghelo **83)** Circolo all Buona Forchetta **85)** Muro

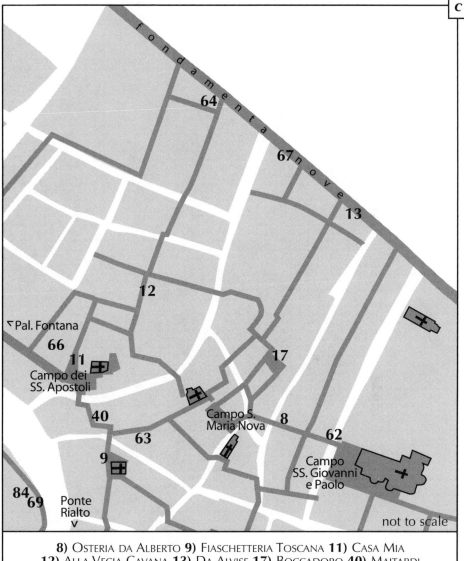

c

8) Osteria da Alberto 9) Fiaschetteria Toscana 11) Casa Mia
12) Alla Vecia Cavana 13) Da Alvise 17) Boccadoro 40) Maitardi
62) Osteria al Ponte 63) Un Mondo diVino 64) Tortuga Pub
66) Ai Promessi Sposi 67) Algiubagio 69) Bancogiro 84) Al Marca

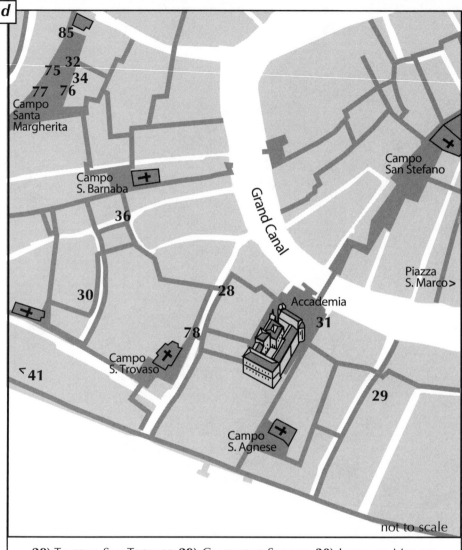

d

85

75 32
34
77 76

Campo
Santa
Margherita

Campo
S. Barnaba

Campo
San Stefano

36

Grand Canal

30 28

Accademia

31

Piazza
S. Marco >

78

Campo
S. Trovaso

< 41

29

Campo
S. Agnese

not to scale

28) TAVERNA SAN TROVASO 29) CANTINONE STORICO 30) LOCANDA MONTIN
31) PIZZERIA ACCADEMIA 32) PIER DICKENS INN 34) TRATTORIA DUE TORRI
36) CASIN DEI NOBILI 41) RIVIERA 75) IL CAFFE 76) MARGUERITE DU CHAMP
77) MADIGAN'S PUB 78) CANTINONE GIA SCHIAVI 85) AI DO DRAGHE

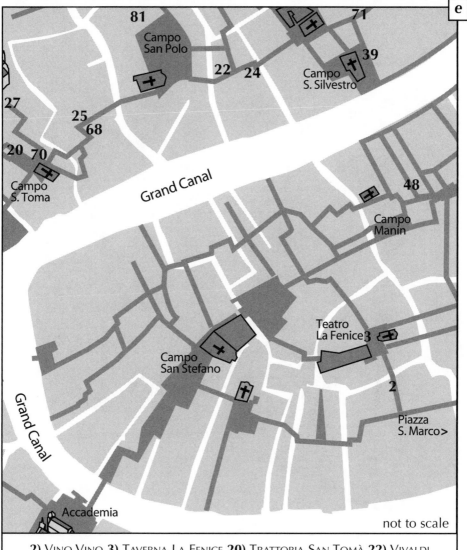

e

81

Campo
San Polo

71

39

Campo
S. Silvestro

22   24

27

25

68

20 70

Campo
S. Toma

Grand Canal

48

Campo
Manin

Teatro
La Fenice 3

Campo
San Stefano

2

Piazza
S. Marco >

Grand Canal

Accademia

not to scale

2) VINO VINO **3)** TAVERNA LA FENICE **20)** TRATTORIA SAN TOMÀ **22)** VIVALDI
24) DA SANDRO **25)** DA IGNAZIO **27)** LA PERLA D'ORIENTE
39) AL PARADISO RISTORANTE **48)** VITAE **68)** BAR AI NOMBOLI
70) CIAK 1 **71)** RUGA RIALTO **81)** ANTICA BIRRERIA

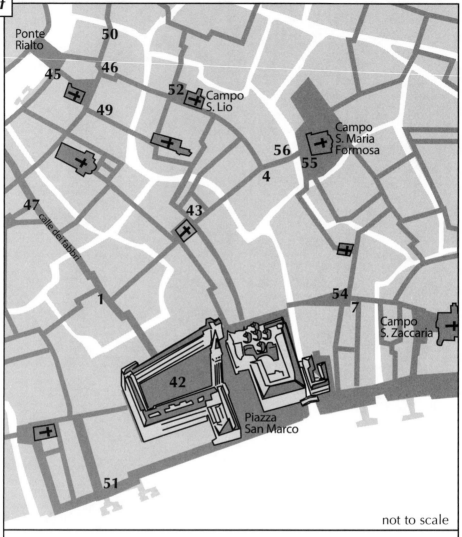

f

Ponte
Rialto

50

45   46

52 Campo
    S. Lio

49

Campo
S. Maria
Formosa

56

55

4

47

calle dei fabbri

43

1

54

7

Campo
S. Zaccaria

42

Piazza
San Marco

51

not to scale

4) ALLE TESTIERE 7) ALLA RIVETTA 42) FLORIAN 43) CAVATAPPI
45) LOWENBRAU BAR 46) ALLA BOTTE 47) MOSCACIEKA 49) DEVIL'S FOREST
50) BACARO JAZZ 51) HARRY'S BAR 52) L'OLANDESE VOLANTE
54) DA BACCO 55) ZANZIBAR 56) INISHARK 1) LE BISTROT DE VENISE

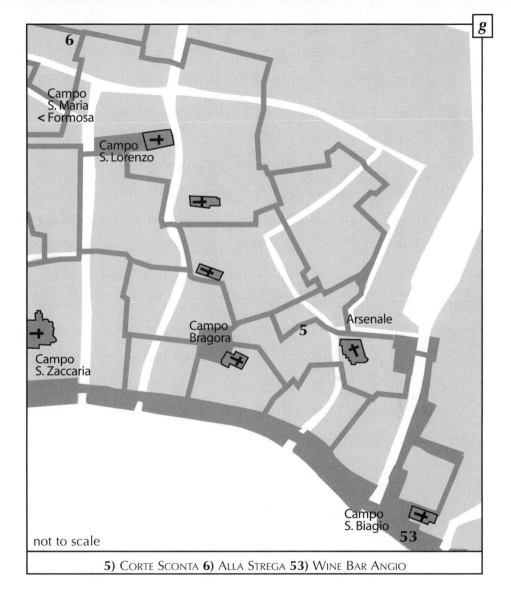

6

Campo
S. Maria
< Formosa

Campo
S. Lorenzo

Campo
Bragora

5

Arsenale

Campo
S. Zaccaria

Campo
S. Biagio

53

not to scale

5) CORTE SCONTA **6)** ALLA STREGA **53)** WINE BAR ANGIO

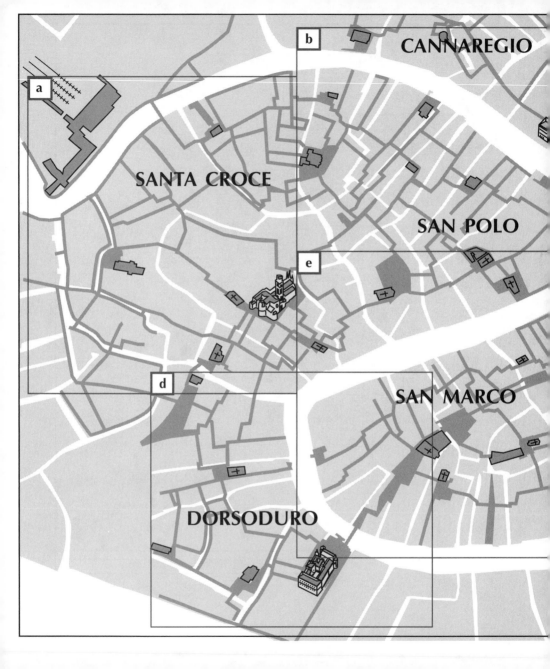

a

b

CANNAREGIO

SANTA CROCE

e

SAN POLO

d

SAN MARCO

DORSODURO

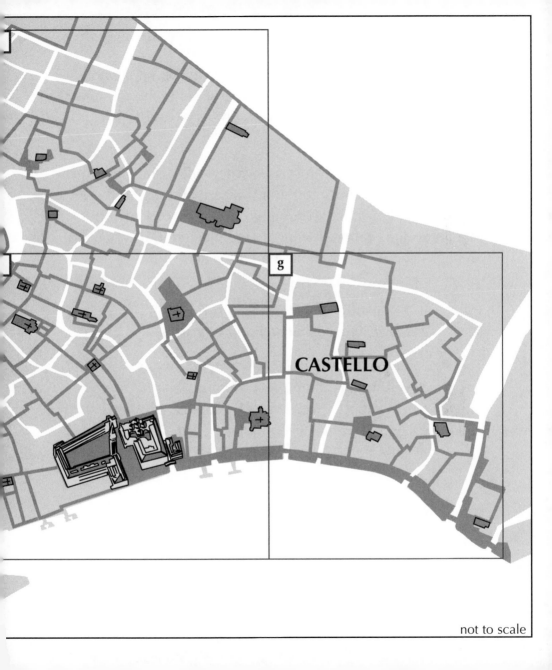

g

CASTELLO

not to scale

Shannon Essa has spent weeks, months, and even a whole year in Venice. Much of this time was spent in the restaurants and bars you will read about here. She now resides in San Diego, California.

Ruth Edenbaum has been in love with Venice since her first visit. She now spends more than two months a year there. Her years of teaching, cooking, writing and reading about food as well as eating in Venice are reflected in this book. She has lived in NJ for more than 30 years.

~~~~~~

As God as your witness, you'll never eat bad food in Venice again.
 - Leslie Dixon, screenwriter and Venice lover

The Slow Travelers community has benefited from the experience and recommendations Shannon and Ruth have provided on Venice restaurants. Now everyone can use this book to make their time in Venice even more special.
 - Pauline Kenny, Slow Travelers *(www.slowtrav.com)*